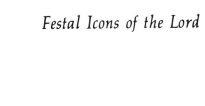

Festal Icons of the Lord

M. Helen Weier, O.S.C.

FESTAL ICONS of the LORD

THE LITURGICAL PRESS
Collegeville, Minnesota

Acknowledgment is gratefully given to: Thomas Drain. "The Cave of the Nativity." *Sacred Signs*, Christmas, 1963. Nicholas of Cusa. *The Vision of God*, trans. Emma Gurney Salter, intro. Evelyn Underhill (New York: Frederick Ungar Publishing Co., 1969). Permission to quote from J.M. Dent & Sons Ltd., London. Joseph Raya and José de Vinck. *Byzantine Daily Worship* (Allendale, New Jersey: Alleluia Press, 1968). Philip Sherrard. "The Art of the Icon," *Sacrament and Image: Essays in the Christian Understanding of Man*, ed. A.M. Allchin (London: The Fellowship of S. Alban and S. Sergius, 1967). Gertrud von Le Fort. *Hymns to the Church*, trans. Margaret Chanler (New York: Sheed and Ward, 1953). Nicholas Zernov. *The Russians and Their Church*, 3rd. ed. (London: S.P.C.K., 1964).

Imprimi potest: Laurene Burns, O.S.C., Abbess, Saint Clare's Monastery, Minneapolis, Minn. *Nihil obstat:* William G. Heidt, O.S.B., S.T.D., *Censor deputatus. Imprimatur:* ✛ George H. Speltz, D.D., Bishop of St. Cloud, October 28, 1977.

ISBN: 0-8146-0967-8

14065

Contents

Foreword

Human beings need symbols. We need signs for our hope and our sustenance. We need vehicles of expression for our inner delights and sorrows, our aspirations and struggles. We need the revelation of the deep beauty surrounding and penetrating our lives. The search for beauty is, in fact, the search for God as revealed to us through Jesus Christ.

A person encountering an icon for the first time may experience ambivalent feelings, a simultaneous attraction and resistance. The profound beauty of an icon is gentle. It does not force its way; it does not intrude. It asks for patience with the uneasiness of early acquaintance. It asks for time spent before it in stillness of gazing. More important, it asks the one praying to allow himself to be gazed upon by it. One must yield space within himself to the icon and its persistent beauty. An icon is prayer and contemplation transformed into art. When exquisite art combines with prayer to become a work of worship and wonder, the art has become sacramental. It manifests to us the God who breaks through all signs and symbols with truth.

From many disciplines people have studied iconography and its place in the Eastern Church. Liturgists, artists, art historians, students of comparative religions, to name but a few, have come with their insights and wisdom, technical knowledge and perspectives. I come to this immense world of beauty as a contemplative religious in the family of Francis and Clare of Assisi. During the past twenty years my community has been enriched through the discovery of the spiritual wealth of the Eastern Churches. Into our celebration of the Eucharist and the Divine Office, we have incorporated music from the Russian Byzantine rite. Icons of the Lord, his Holy Mother, and the saints beautify the walls of our monastery and chapel.

Three years ago, in a desire to discover more of this world of prayer, silence, wonder, and loveliness, I registered at the College of St. Teresa, Winona, Minnesota, for an independent study of the festal icons of the Lord. I pursued this study in our monastery in the daily context of liturgy, private prayer, reading, and work that makes up the rhythm of life in our community. This book is an attempt to share the fruits of this study.

We need symbols and signs to reveal the deep beauty that dwells within us, surrounds us, awaits us, and we need doors into new and holy places. Perhaps this small work will open a door, even so slightly, for the reader—a door into the world of contemplation and joy that is portrayed in iconography.

I will ever hold in grateful remembrance the support, encouragement and help of Sister Helen Rolfson, O.S.F., my study director; my sisters in community, and my family and friends who are in some way co-authors of this work.

Sister M. Helen Weier, O.S.C.

Feast of Our Lady of Sorrows
September 15, 1977

Introduction

"**Y**es, it ceased to wander—it stayed until the church was closed for good. People worshipped it and said their most heartfelt prayers to it. Well they might, for it wasn't just holy, it was mercilessly beautiful, too. There's never been such beauty." I was struck by Pasha's phrase "mercilessly beautiful": she had meant, no doubt, to refer to the "Merciful Virgin," but had got confused in her expressions. Yet, I reflected, all beauty is power—an absolute, indestructible power, which either throws you at its feet or lifts you up to itself. Beauty is that which we cannot resist, and therefore it is indeed merciless.

Yes, such a beauty as never was on earth.[1]

The aged peasant Pasha speaks of her memories of a wonder-working icon that existed in a small Russian village. According to the story surrounding its origin, the icon first appeared in the mud by a clear, cold spring. Three times the village priest rescued it from the ravine and took it to his church; three times it disappeared through locked doors. Pasha tells how the local villagers then escorted the icon with dignity from the spring to the church. After this procession the miraculous icon "ceased to wander" and the Virgin filled the church with her "merciless beauty." The icon of the Vladimir Mother of God is not the "Merciful Virgin" of Pasha's account, but it possesses the same merciless beauty. Under her gaze, I dedicate this book to her honor and that of her divine Son. I like to think that in this most tender of icons, heaven touches earth and draws us nearer to the eternal beauty—that beauty upon which we shall gaze forever in the call to dwell in the heart of the Father, the Son, and their Spirit of love.

Festal Icons of the Lord

Chapter 1

Eastern Iconography

The icon may be a beautiful art form, but for the Eastern Church it is much more than that. Just as the Greek Orthodox Church traditionally thinks of itself as a reflection on earth of the heavenly kingdom, similarly, the icon is a sacred, consecrated object. The West treats the icon as an edifying picture; the East regards it as a redeeming mystery, a window through which to look into the world transcending time and space, a work that is a continuation of the life of the Christian on earth. The icon inspires and instructs; it makes present the holy one depicted there; it is a channel for divine grace to pass to the worshipper.

"Icon," a Greek word meaning "image, representation," indicates more specifically a religious image painted according to a conventional model or symbolism. Christian art has among its forebears Egyptian funereal art and ancient Greek art. From the scattered pieces of truth found in that art, the Church adopted what was of its own, all that was "Christian before Christ." It was the ancient Egyptian tomb portraits, distinguished by their fixed, direct gaze, immobile faces and large eyes that became a model for Byzantine iconographers. Gradually the Byzantines developed their own wholly Christian language of iconography. Under the Grand Duke Vladimir in the tenth century, Russia accepted the Greek Orthodox faith as the religion of the emerging Russian empire; the art of Byzantium was part of the inheritance. Russian artists, having apprenticed under Greek iconographers, gave a national complexion to the art. Indeed the art of the icon reached a peak in Russia unknown in any other country.

Today we take for granted images of the holy God and his saints. It is necessary to recall that there was a time in the history of the Church—in the eighth and ninth centuries—when the very existence of images of holy people, and most especially of Christ, was questioned and challenged as being blasphemous and idolatrous. The storm raged so fiercely that the combat taxed the ingenuity of the best theologians of the time. Perhaps it would be helpful to review the Iconoclast controversy and its basic assumptions.

Through zeal for the pure worship of God and veneration of his saints, the Iconoclasts set themselves as destroyers of images. Those images that existed at the time of the Edict of the Iconoclasts in Constantinople in 730 were destroyed in great numbers and the production of new images was forbidden. On what assumptions did this sect base its conclusions? First, the Iconoclasts claimed that the deity cannot be represented or painted in an image. The God of the Old Testament is invisible, transcendent, unable to be depicted. The ancient Hebrews preserved this concept of their God by forbidding the creation of any image or likeness of *anything* on earth or in heaven which might become a substitute for the truth. The Iconoclasts returned to this proscription and thus turned back the pages of Christian history, maintaining that if Christ is God, he is also unable to be depicted. In their fervor they denounced as blasphemous both the painter and the devout worshipper. The Acts of Nicaea, 787, stated:

> The divine nature is completely uncircumscribable and cannot be depicted or presented by artists in any medium whatsoever. The word Christ means both God and man, and an icon of Christ would therefore have to be an image of God in the flesh of the Son of God. But this is impossible. The artist would fall either into the heresy which claims that the divine and human natures of Christ are separate or into that which holds that there is only one nature in Christ.[2]

Secondly, the Iconoclasts argued that there is no distinction between the image and the original. On the other hand, the Orthodox Christians saw a very real distinction between them: image and original are not consubstantial, are not of the same substance. The heretics also adopted the view that the Church possessed but one authentic image of Christ in his incarnate state of living among us, that image being in the Body and Blood of the Eucharist and in that alone. Finally, the opponents of images argued from the purist point of view that holy men and women ought not to be painted; their only genuine image was the embodiment of their virtues. They concluded that the only image of them to be made by others was the daily portrayal of their virtues in Christian imitation.

The whole argument of the Iconoclasts, with their charges of idolatry and blasphemy, was rendered powerless by the Church's strong distinction between the material image and the person depicted there: the image and the original are two distinct things. The Council of Nicaea, 787, carefully differentiated worship and veneration. Worship is due to God alone and in no way to an image of wood or a painted picture. Veneration is due to an image by reason of the person it depicts, not because of the wood or the paint.

The storms of the Iconoclastic period have brought forth profound theological explanations of iconography that the world might never have received otherwise. Basic themes of Christianity were at stake in this struggle: the doctrines of the incarnation and redemption and the Christian view of matter and material creation. For the Eastern Christians the supreme justification of the icon lies in the truth of the incarnation, the taking of a material body by the Second Person of the Blessed Trinity. The incarnation is "that great act of self-portraiture"[3] of the Son. St. John of Damascus develops this idea:

> Of old, God the incorporeal and uncircumscribed, was not depicted at all. But now that God has appeared in the flesh and lived among men, I make an image of the

God who can be seen. I do not worship matter, but I worship the Creator of matter, who for my sake became material and deigned to dwell in matter, who through matter effected my salvation. I will not cease from worshipping the matter through which my salvation has been effected.[4]

When men saw Christ on earth, they saw God face to face. By the denial of iconographic representation, the Iconoclasts rejected the very existence of the incarnation in history, rejected, as well, the place in Christianity of material things. Thus the icon has come to mean much more than a mere art piece, more than a visual aid or substitute for the written word to help the illiterate. It holds in itself a vital, all-important expression of truth beyond what verbal language alone can say. Whereas both the written word and the image teach us the truths of Scripture and tradition, the image excels in leading us into the ways of prayer and communion with God.

From its very beginning Christian art had the character of elucidating the message in the Old and New Testaments, a disclosure of truth in graphic or plastic form. The essential concern of the artist was to transmit the message faithfully. For this purpose he had need to use all of created nature, so vast is the good news, so immense the world of the Spirit. Man needs an expression of God, and even though this God be expressed in every medium possible, he yet remains the unknowable, the deeply hidden one.

Some of the earliest Christian art is in the catacombs. The symbolic art found there does not depict the problems of life but attempts to answer those problems with the gospel teaching. Such spiritual realities cannot be presented but by symbols. Consequently, at the time of Roman suppression and martyrdom, Christian art showed not the sufferings of the martyrs but the attitude of the Christian toward these sufferings. After the Peace of Constantine in 313 brought the Church out of the catacombs and established her in legal existence in the empire, converts joined in great numbers.

Many of them, however, could not comprehend the meaning of the Christian symbolism that had been in use since the earliest years of Christianity. To enable the converts to grasp the teachings of the Church, pictorial art came into use in addition to the symbolic. In the fourth and fifth centuries large murals of Old and New Testament events began to appear in places of worship. In order to give yet further expression to her teachings, the Church at this time established many major feasts. Celebrations of these feasts afforded opportunities for the development of all the arts.

Icon painters of the Eastern Church worked according to canons or rules consisting of patterns for painting the various events in the lives of the Lord, his Mother, and the saints. The artist receded behind anonymity; the importance of the work lay, not in the man doing the work, but rather in the message of truth it was to bear to Christians. Some icons are patterned on material found in the Apocrypha, namely, those books from early Christian times which are not included in the canon of Sacred Scripture. The word "apocryphal" meant "hidden"—*apocryphos* in Greek. Some writings, it was thought, were too sacred, too secret, to be known to the public at large; only initiates to the new Way might have access to them. However, the word gradually took on another meaning: spurious, false, illegitimate. In order that their works might receive acceptance, the Apocrypha authors attached to their writings the name of one or the other apostle or close disciple of the Lord.[5]

Despite the specious element, the Apocrypha were of considerable significance to the icon painter and the Church historian for information regarding customs and trends proper to the beginning years of Christian belief. An example is the Protoevangelium of James which has influenced liturgy, literature, and art through the centuries. It is the source of the cult of Joachim and Anna, the holy parents of the Mother of God. The feast of the Presentation of the Virgin in the temple has its source there, as do many legends about the Blessed Virgin.

In the Eastern Church iconographic art and the Divine Liturgy grew side by side. The image joined with liturgy conveys the gospel teachings and those of sacred tradition. The gospels and the icon are two facets of the one truth, the former written, the latter visual, both in a deep and mutual correspondence. As one of the forms of revelation and knowledge of God, the icon ranks with the Cross and the Word in Scripture.

It follows that from its very nature Church art is a liturgic art. Its liturgic character is not due to the fact that the image serves as a framework and addition to the divine service, but to their mutual correspondence. The mystery enacted and the mystery depicted are one, both inwardly in their meaning and outwardly in the symbolism which expresses this meaning.[6]

The icon and its relation to the liturgy is summarized in Philip Sherrard's article "The Art of the Icon":

> We have become accustomed to looking at works of art as independent entities, areas of line and colour cut off from surrounding space, enclosed in a frame and hung upon a wall. An icon, if it is to be regarded as an icon, is not something which can be separated off in this fashion. On the contrary, it is something whose full nature cannot be understood unless it is seen in relationship to the organic whole of the spiritual structure of which it forms a part. Divorced from this whole, hung in a frame upon a wall, and looked at as an individual aesthetic object, it is divorced from the context in which it can function as an icon. It may then be an attractive piece of decoration, but as an icon it ceases to exist. For as an icon it can only exist within the particular framework of belief and worship to which it belongs. An icon divorced from the framework ceases to be an icon. An icon divorced from a place and act of worship is a contradiction in terms.[7]

It would be unreal to think that only saints could or did paint icons, as we know the Church is made up of saints *and* sinners. Yet the luxuriant source for this sacred art is the Spirit; the more perfectly the artist is in touch with this Spirit by contemplation and freedom as a son of God, the purer will be his work. Richard Hare in *The Art and Artists of Russia*[8] says that the iconographer stands between man and his God as visual intermediary, a high and lofty role. Many iconographers were monks. The most important requirement of such an artist's life was that he be very much in the stream of the Church's sacramental and ascetical life. The canons demanded that the artist prepare himself for his work by prayer and fasting, the confession of his sins, Holy Communion—in general, by purity and humility of life. The power that man has to make images is a share in the all-powerful creativity of God; man uses this gift to the extent of his ability and in a manner appropriate to his nature, mirroring something of the inexhaustible originality of our God.

In following fixed prescriptions concerning each icon's portrayal, the painter's role could be seen as analogous to the priest's officiating at the worship of the faithful. While both priest and artist conform to rubrics laid down for their celebrations, yet each necessarily officiates at his office according to his natural gifts and endowments, his character and technical proficiency, his creative transposition of the given rules. In iconography the personal element is quite subtle when compared with that expressed in other arts; yet close observation of any two icons of the same subject and done by different artists bears out personal expression.

The theology of icons lies principally in three doctrines: the transfiguration of man by grace, the existence of the spiritual world, and the re-creation of all things in the Lord Jesus. The ordinary rules of realistic art to which we are accustomed suffer what seems to be violence at the hands of the iconographer; if and when this occurs, it is in the service of the foregoing doctrines. The organs of sense, as well as other details such as hair and clothing, are put in the service of the general harmony of the icon, and with the whole body of the saint are united in one ascending movement Godward. The icon

> . . . does not eliminate anything human; it does not exclude either the psychological or the worldly element. . . just as in the Holy Scriptures, the whole load of human thoughts, feelings, and knowledge is represented in the icon at its point of contact with the world of Divine Grace, and in this contact all that is not purified is burnt up as by fire. Every manifestation of human nature acquires meaning, becomes illumined, finds its true place and significance.[9]

Portraying the transfiguration of man by grace, all is brought into supreme harmony; disorder is an attribute of *fallen* man. The external senses participate in the transfiguration in glory; the nose and lips are small and pinched-looking, while the over-sized eyes have no glint in them. This is the artist's way of stating that the person in glory has knowledge now which comes directly from the vision of God, no longer through the mediation of the outward senses. The coloring of the flesh, often a copper tint, and the look of radiancy and inner light also point to the character of spiritualization. One of the tasks of the icon is to guide the emotions and faculties of human nature on the road toward transfiguration.

In iconography one will never find "still life" scenes or paintings of scenery for their own sake. The plant and animal worlds in the Eastern iconographer's art do not hold a place apart from man; they participate in man's redemption; they take part in the peace and order of an harmonious whole. The holiness of man has a personal, as well as a general human and cosmic, significance. Icons point to the future unity of all things in the new heavens and the new earth, when even the sun will surrender its role to the light of the Lamb on his throne. One will not find in icons any source of light, such as the sun or a candle; it is divine light that floods the icon, that light which is the background of the icon.

In its almost grotesque portrayal, architecture is difficult to understand in this iconography:

> Architecture plays a peculiar role of its own in the icon. While it serves, as does landscape, to denote that the event depicted in the icon is in truth connected historically with a definite place, it never *contains this event inside itself* [emphasis mine], but merely serves as a background to it, for, according to the very meaning of the icon, the action is not enclosed in or limited to a particular place, just as while being manifested in time, it is not limited to a certain time. Thus a scene which takes place inside a building is always shown as taking place with the building as background. . . . With rare exceptions, the human figure is always constructed correctly—everything is in its right place. The same applies to the clothes: their details, the folds, etc., are perfectly logical. But architecture, both in form and grouping is often contrary to human logic and in separate details is emphatically illogical. Doors and windows are often pierced in wrong places, their size does not correspond to their functions, etc. . . . The meaning of this phenomenon is that architecture is the only element in the icon with the help of which it is possible to show clearly that the action taking place before our eyes is outside the laws of human logic, outside the laws of earthly existence (Ouspensky, p. 41).

The icon painter works with honest materials which represent the fullest participation of the vegetable, animal, and mineral worlds in the creation of an icon. These materials are used in their natural forms, the painter himself preparing them for the process. Wood must be very choice, well-seasoned and aged, not subject to warping. From the wood the artist gouges a space, a holy space in which to work his sacred task. While the frame and the lateral stave are meant to help resist the warping process, the edge also allows the artist to rest his hand while working without touching the paint.

The artist knows his materials well. Natural organic materials of which he knows both the good and the bad qualities are what he uses: egg yolk, water, vinegar (or fig tree juice in Italy, beer in Germany), linen, alabaster or chalk, glue made of gelatin, mineral pigments, linseed oil, resins—and each of these substances in very specific proportions and ratio. Oil paints were not accepted by the iconographers until the "period of decadence" in the eighteenth century, the reason being, says Ouspensky, "that, owing to their sensual character, oil paints are unfit to express the asceticism, spiritual richness and joy belonging to an icon" (p. 55). The crown of the entire process of making an icon is the celebration of its blessing, its baptism.

With the smoke of incense and candles burning before the holy icons, over the years the brilliant colors gradually give way to soot and darkness. Instead of cleaning the icon, the owner of the treasure would perhaps commission another artist to paint approximately over the original image. Four or five paintings might obscure the beauty of the original after many decades. The restoration and cleaning of icons is a very meticulous and delicate labor, undertaken only by experts who often can uncover images which have been painted over several times. When cleaned, the original colors may prove as amazingly brilliant as when painted two, six, or eight centuries ago.

Icon painters employ many means to indicate the glorification in another world of Christ, his Mother, and the saints. Yet the icon is a direct address to the world of the worshippers, not cut off from the world outside itself and the mysteries it contains. Here we recall the creativity of the glance of God, the "Absolute Glance,"[10] that excludes nothing from its view.

The principle of frontality is operative in true Byzantine iconography; the holy one is pictured either full face or three-fourths face toward the worshipper. Profile, on the other hand, is already the beginning of absence, and it begins to break communion. Gervase Mathew points out in *Byzantine Aesthetics* that only such figures as those with whom the worshipper would wish to make no contact, for example, Judas at the betrayal of Jesus, are shown in profile.[11]

The heads of many figures seem to be pushed up from the back, and the icons themselves seem to have flat backgrounds; that is, the eye sees the figure or figures but nothing further back. Inverse perspective, making the worshipper himself the vanishing point, has the same effect of restraining the eye and makes it unable to penetrate, unable to enter into the image in any depth. This principle gives a person the sense that it is truly *I* who am encountering this holy one in the image, concentrating on the image itself in direct confrontation, the only possibility. When art leads the faithful to this direct confrontation with God, to this deeper grasp of the ultimate meaning of life, then it is truly sacramental.

The fifteenth-century mystic Nicholas of Cusa devotes himself in *The Vision of God or the Icon* to the contemplation of the universal yet particular, perfect, unchanging gaze of God, a look that is literally creative. Evelyn Underhill in the introduction to that work writes:

> God, for Nicholas, is "in the very truth an Unlimited Sight"; the Absolute Glance falls equally, simultaneously and unflickeringly on all. Within this Perfect Vision the small life of man is lived; it conditions his limited spiritual experience. Only because God first looks at him, can man desire to look at God; for the finite in all its degrees is enfolded and conditioned by the Infinite (pp. xii-xiii).

Nicholas' own words elaborate on this universal glance:

> . . . while I look on this pictured face, whether from the east or from the west or south, it seems in like manner itself to look on me, and after the same fashion, according as I move my face, that face seemeth turned toward me. . . . each of you shall find that from whatsoever quarter he regardeth it, it looketh upon him as if it looked on none other. . . .

And, as he knoweth from the icon to be fixed and unmoved, he will marvel at the motion of its immovable gaze. . . .

> Thy being, Lord, letteth not go of my being. I exist in that measure in which Thou art with me, and, since Thy look is Thy being, I *am* [emphasis mine] because Thou dost look at me, and if Thou didst turn Thy glance from me I should cease to be (pp. 15, 16, 24).

Icons render present in some way the reality they portray. We hear stories of the power of icons, of miracle-working icons. Where does this power come from?

> If the icon could be seen as a focal point through which the devotion paid before it was transferred to the original, then it could be argued that the converse would be true, that the original could act through the icon, even in a certain sense be present in it.[12]

It is divine grace which transfigures man so that he comes to more and more mature adulthood in Christ. Icons are a "sign of the triumph of God's grace over the dark elements in matter and in man's heart, and the restoration of the true order of creation."[13] Through the gaze of God cast upon the world through and in the incarnation, man receives the power to become a living icon of God. It is this transfiguration of man, rather than an exact portrait of this or that person, which underlies the significance of the icon.

"He was transfigured before them, and his face shone like the sun, and his garments became white as light" (Matthew 17:2). The whole body of the Lord was bathed in light, a light foreshadowing that light which would transfigure him in the glory of his resurrection and his ascension to the right hand of the Father. Whatever the body of the Lord experienced in his earthly existence, that to *some* degree becomes in *some* manner the experience of that body which he constituted as his bride, the Church. If we stop short at considering the merely historical events of Christ's life, we miss the full significance and mystery of the same events in their meaning for all people of all times. For a fuller discussion of the mystery of transfiguration in the life of man on earth, see the reflection on the feast of the Transfiguration of the Lord later in this work.

Annually the Orthodox Church keeps a

Sunday of the Triumph of Orthodoxy which was inaugurated to celebrate the victory over Iconoclasm in the year 842. One of the collect-hymns in the liturgy for that day summarizes the doctrinal significance of sacred icons:

> The indefinable word of the Father made himself definable, having taken flesh of thee, O Mother of God, and, having refashioned the soiled image to its former estate, has suffused it with Divine beauty. But confessing salvation we show it forth in deed and word.[14]

This is indeed a precise and exact statement of the meaning of the icon. As observed, the icon is based on the doctrine of the incarnation. The Lord, the God-Man, had a representable Mother while at the same time he had an unrepresentable Father. This fact affirms and explains the use of image. To deny the human image of the Savior is to deny that he is the fruit of divine motherhood. Because there was incarnation, there is need for icons, for images. Although attempts have been made, no one has successfully portrayed the Father and the Spirit according to human form; no one has seen them: had anyone looked upon them in the flesh at any point in history, there would have been need to represent them in image as we do the Son, the Incarnate Word of the Trinity. So firmly was the doctrine of images bound up with the very tenets of the faith that, for the defense of sacred images, steadfast and unwavering Christians went to torture and death during the Iconoclast heresy.

The first part of the liturgical collect quoted above is based on *the* icon, the Lord Jesus; the next part relates to man's power and vocation to be an icon in turn. Man in the world is called to be a living image of the Lord whose name he bears, the Lord who has given him a share in his own divine life through baptism. Even though one may have sinned, he yet bears this image of God. In the Order for the Burial of the Dead for a lay person, these words are sung:

> I am an image of thy glory ineffable, though I bear the brands of transgressions. Show thy compassions upon thy creature, O Master, and purify me by thy loving-kindness; grant unto me the home-country of my heart's desire, making me again a citizen of paradise.

Then in the hand of the deceased Christian is placed an icon of the Savior: he who bore his image on earth is now departed to behold him face to face in blessedness.

All creation is gathered up into the cosmic redemption that follows upon man's return to his true likeness. Every creature by reason of its creation by almighty God has a splendor shed upon it by its Maker, each in its own way and measure. In other words, everything—man and animal, plant and inorganic creation—*everything* God made shares in the divine beauty and has upon it the seal of the Lord. This beauty expresses itself simply as the beauty belonging to the creature as creature: to the rose as rose, to the bird as bird, to the rock as rock. St. Paul tells us:

> Ever since the creation of the world his invisible nature, namely his eternal power and deity, has been clearly perceived in the things that have been made (Rom. 1:20).

Leonid Ouspensky, considering beauty as an attribute of the kingdom of God, points to the possibilities of transfiguration that lie in all creatures:

> The beauty of the visible world lies not in the transitory splendor of its present state, but in the very meaning of its existence, in its coming transfiguration laid down in it as a possibility to be realised by man. In other words, beauty is holiness, and its radiance the participation of the creature in Divine Beauty (p. 36).

The icon has no independent existence; its purpose is solely to reflect divine beauty. As we gaze upon the merciless beauty of an exquisite icon, we know then that its value lies not only, or even primarily, in its beauty in itself; it truly shows us something of infinite radiance and splendor.

Chapter 2

Russian Iconography

Here this study transposes to a Russian key, emphasizing the Russian icon and treating briefly its historical origins and development. This will also lead to a few comments on the spirituality and the ways of looking at iconography through the large soul of the Russian people.

The monk Rublev's "The Savior," an icon that shows the toll that time can take upon such works, introduces us into the finest of Russian iconography and opens, as well, our discussion of specifically Russian works, techniques, and spiritual views. Gazing upon "The Savior" and being gazed upon by it, one recalls the words of Nicholas of Cusa—*the glance of the Lord falls equally, simultaneously and unwaveringly upon all.* But one must take the time to contemplate the Holy Face. It is a sermon in color and form; it is prayer enthroned on wood. This is true of all icons, those masterpieces which for the Russian people and for us are points of contact with the world of divine realities. In them the nearness of merciful grace becomes almost tangible.

The Russians have a characteristic way of approaching spiritual realities and their pictorial representation. A contemporary writer remarks that the Russian saint is

> ... the son of a special people, having as such his own special natural features and his own special historical path determining his origins, his culture, and the world in which he lives. Berdyaev is right when he says that there exists a by no means accidental connection between the geography of a soul and plain geography.... The image of this Russian soul and her spiritual features are determined amidst enormous, monotonous plains, boundless distances where measureless infinite, the supernatural, make up, as it were, part of every day existence. Spacious, like her native land, the Russian soul knows no boundaries.[15]

As an aid toward understanding and appreciating the icons of Russia, it might be helpful to look briefly at the historical setting in which they were born. Legend has it that St. Andrew the Apostle came to Russia in the first century to preach Christ and his resurrection. The unlettered inhabitants forgot most of the essentials, remembering only the doctrine of immortality and the Sign of the Cross. Then around 955 Christianity returned to the land through its first queen, Olga, who had become a Christian. At that time the new religion had little appeal to the people; in fact, the queen's son Sviatoslav, the next ruler, violently rejected the faith. It was Queen Olga's grandson, Vladimir of Kiev, who took steps to establish a universal religion, Greek Orthodox Christianity. Vladimir is honored by the Church as "holy equal-of-the-apostles."

The inhabitants of the wide-open spaces were a difficult people to bring under one central authority. Duke Vladimir found it politically advantageous to command obedience by means of energetic measures and rules. Although he may well have had many a devout moment in his decision-making process, he saw one unifying force as a power for controlling a then undisciplined people and as a panacea for their ills. In 988, Duke Vladimir went in search of a single universal religion. He sent envoys across the known world who were to report to the duke their impressions of the religions they encountered. The Greek Orthodox Church seemed, from all reports, to be the best suited to the role of a unitary religion.

The characteristic Russian thoroughness in conversion and the speed of adjustment to Christian Orthodoxy was not wholly due to Vladimir's decrees; it so happened that this new religion appealed very much to the innate love of the Russian people for splendor, magnificence, and beauty of ritual. Whereas Christianity had been introduced into Russia long before the tenth century, the edict of Christian baptism for all in 988 marks its official acceptance. Alongside the new Christianity lingered dark remembrances of pre-Christian practices. Yet the Church, coming to the Russians, did not efface the national character. Elements that were reconcilable with Christian dogma and ethic she accepted, thus forging strong foundations in Christian Russia. Until the time of Peter the Great in the 1700s, Russia knew no rift between religious and secular culture; no renaissance had as yet suggested that man himself was the measure of all things.

With the coming of Christianity, the Russians inherited the art of Byzantium as well as its faith and ritual. Artists, liturgists, and priests came to Russia at the request—or better, the command—of Vladimir; at the same time he ordered the destruction of all pagan objects of worship and art. Gradually the Russian people began to apprentice under the foreign masters; the art and architecture that came with Christianity quickly found their place for they were congenial to the Russian people who soon began to express themselves and their beliefs in the new style. Working in the structure inherited from the Byzantines, they laid the foundations for a national iconographic art, finally coming to the maturation of specifically Russian painting. By the thirteenth and fourteenth centuries a style had arisen that we can identify as Russian; this happened primarily under the monk Andrei Rublev, who breathed a new spirit into the Byzantine forms.

Russia was not bound, as was Byzantium, by a complex inheritance of cultural antiquity. She was a relatively young country and rapidly came to a level of purity and excellence in iconography that made her outstanding. Whereas it was the claim of Byzantium to be preeminent in transmitting theology through word, it is the glory of Russia to excel in giving the world theology through image. From the advent of Christianity until the time of Peter the Great, Russia had only a few writers in theology but many iconographers.

The asceticism that characterizes Russian icons accents the joy and lightness of the Lord's yoke; these images possess a childlike carefreeness, peace, and delight: the "Russian icon is the highest expression in art of god-like humility" (Ouspensky, p. 46). Russian painters

> . . . were bent exclusively on inner vision which the contemplation of divine beings and sacred histories aroused in them. . . . Like the musical composer, the Russian artist stretched and moulded the inherited material to fit the peculiar stresses of his personal feeling. . . . Here, then, is an art which in its main characteristics is singularly free from all the mechanism of representation, purified, like music, of all but its direct appeals to the spirit. . . .
>
> The Western artist has always felt the need of keeping to a constant frame of reference, so to speak. If he constructs a space, it must be a space of the same kind throughout, and he hastens to discover the laws of perspective which express that consistency, and having found them, he applies them throughout. . . . His imagery is governed by the idea of causal relations.
>
> Now, to the Russian artist, causality is unknown. The world of his imagination is under no causal constraints—it is indeed professedly an entirely miraculous world, where anything may happen at any moment.[16]

About the Russian sense of the miraculous in the world, Metropolitan Anthony Bloom writes:

> A miracle is not something which is marvelous, although it appears so to us; a miracle is the normal relationship between God and his world, the supple, live, loving relationship there can be between what God has made, capable of knowing him, of hearing him, and himself.[17]

There is in the native Russian soul a deep thirst for the cosmic transfiguration of all things. Their classic iconographic art shows forth this longing. For them their icons are

> . . . dynamic manifestations of man's spiritual power to redeem creation through beauty and art. . . . the artists aimed at demonstrating that men, animals and plants, and the whole cosmos could be rescued from their present state of degradation and restored to their proper "Image." The [icons] were pledges of the coming victory of a redeemed creation over the fallen one . . . . for in man and through man the whole Universe was restored to its proper purpose: the glorification of its Creator. . . . for the Russians the artistic perfection of an ikon was not only a reflection of the celestial glory—it was a concrete example of matter restored to its original harmony and beauty, and serving as a vehicle of the Spirit. The ikons were part of the transfigured cosmos and, therefore, they could uplift the spirit of man and assist human beings in their struggle against disunity, disease and death.[18]

The Russian iconographers painted with the understanding that one of the deepest meanings of the icon, the transfiguration of all things in the new heavens and the new earth, is conveyed through its coloring. For example, the thin lines of gold that spin their way across the pictures serve to remind us of the light of the heavenly Spirit pervading all things. They also looked upon the icon as a place of sanctifying forces, not of beautiful forms in repose and rest. Their sacred art holds a space for man's communion with God. A contemporary daughter of Russia, Professor Irene Posnoff, develops this idea:

> The Christian view of the world cannot be separated from the worship of ethical beauty which appears like a lively and not an abstract truth. . . . liturgical and iconographical beauty is intended to be a kind of revelation of the beauty of God that a Christian must find reproduced again in creatures. To a loving eye, spiritually transfigured, the world also appears transfigured, and the beauty of God is seen in creatures. Everything is transformed in the Incarnation and Redemption of Christ. Such is the basic idea of the Orthodox Church, writes Arseniev, when he explains the sympathy of the Russian for St. Francis of Assisi, who embodies exactly this essential aspect of Eastern Christianity.[19]

From the viewpoint of art, the Russian icons are treasures; until the beginning of this century it seems that Russia herself was unaware that she had some of the world's most beautiful masterpieces. This occurred because her people regarded their icons not primarily as works of art but rather as holy, sacred images inseparable from the Divine Liturgy, the worship of God, and the veneration of his holy Mother and the saints.

When a restoration plan took effect and experts learned the art of cleaning icons without destroying the original beauty, many works were revealed that were previously unknown to the Russian people and to the outside world. In 1913 the first large-scale exhibition of the better icons took place in Moscow. It is small wonder, then, that so late in the history of these masterpieces the western world has become aware of them.

During the Russian Revolution in 1917, when churches were closed and barred or turned into grain storage bins or carpenters' workshops, many icons were destroyed or simply left to decay. The more famous ones were removed to art galleries where many Christians of the silent Church today return again and again to pay their muted homage before these holy images in exile. Many renowned icons played important parts in the national history of the country; it would have been an act of sheer violence for the revolutionaries to destroy these holy signs of God's presence.

Three Russian artists of great fame in the medieval period should receive our attention. The first of these in time was Theophanes the Greek (1330-1405). He came to Russia, working in Novgorod and later at the Monastery of the Trinity at Zagorsk in the latter half of the fourteenth century. "The Greek" became as true a Russian artist as El Greco had in his time become a Spanish one. Tamara Rice says of Theophanes that he had little of tenderness and nothing of sweetness in his work, yet he is hailed as one of Europe's outstanding painters because of his bold and spirited style as well as the expression of intense inner life in his figures.

The monk-iconographer in whom Russia reached its artistic zenith was Andrei Rublev (ca. 1370-1430), a student of Theophanes. Rublev had the soul of a contemplative and of a keenly perceptive artist. Out of that nobility of soul he was to enrich the culture of the Middle Ages with some of its greatest artistic achievements. His flowing yet decisive style and his elimination

of the non-essential set a standard which many artists of Moscow tried to emulate. Even during his lifetime Rublev's preeminence was recognized among his people; indeed, so outstanding an artist was this monk that the public annals of Russia noted the loss of any of his icons as an event of national consequence. We find in his work an almost total absence of shadow: the light of God allows no shadow to stand out for he is "the Father of lights with whom there is no variation or shadow due to change"(James 1:17).

In the late fourteenth century a holy man named Sergius of Radonezh founded Trinity Monastery (later known as Trinity-St. Sergius) at Zagorsk near Moscow. The monastery eventually became an important center of icon painting in all of Russia as Sergius encouraged this art in particular. He commissioned workshops to be set up in the monastery and assigned some monks to learn the art. In tribute to this Abbot Sergius, who had a profound influence on the spiritual and cultural life of Russia, Andrei Rublev's abbot commissioned him to begin work on his most outstanding piece, "The Hospitality of Abraham," more commonly known as "The Old Testament Trinity."

The third great iconographer of the period was Dionysius (ca. 1440-1505). He based his art to some extent on the Rublev tradition. While some critics see in his work a delicacy that is synonymous with weakness and that seems to foreshadow the decline that gradually came over iconography, yet his prolific work is forceful, having about it a great dignity and serenity. Dionysius expanded the subject matter of Russian art by representing many of the miracles of Christ.

Under the anti-clerical Peter the Great (1672-1725), the deterioration of the traditional style of Russian iconography began. The dogmatic content of the icon gradually vanished from the people's awareness. To iconographers who had come under the influence of the West, symbolic realism became a language incomprehensible. The old style lingered on only as a craft, though occasionally a work of great merit was created. For the most part a whole era in the history of classical iconography had passed.

Chapter 3

The Place of Icons in Church and Home

We have seen that an icon exists rightfully as an icon only in the framework of worship and belief. Prior to the fifteenth century, icons were mainly in the larger churches. Later, small private chapels imitated the practice. Gradually, as people became more prosperous, personal ownership of icons grew more common until every believer's home became the shrine of at least one icon. Let us look first at the use of icons in churches.

The early Fathers saw symbolic meaning in the church building itself. The church is the image both of the immaterial world and the sensory world, of the spiritual and the physical man. The sanctuary symbolizes the first, the immaterial and the spiritual; the nave symbolizes the sensory, the physical. Yet, each area of the church constitutes, with the other, part of the whole, the first nourishing and enlightening the second, with the latter becoming a sensory manifestation of the former.

The ceiling with the open dome represents heaven. From the dome of the church the figure of Christ the Pantocrator, Ruler of all, looks down from heaven upon the assembled faithful and hears their prayers as he reminds them of his omnipresence. The floor of the building represents this world, where a pilgrim people makes its way to heaven. Stairs lead to the altar which stands higher than floor level. The altar is, as it were, suspended between heaven and earth, lifting the faithful up to heaven through the Word of the gospels and the grace of the sacraments.

Between the nave and the sanctuary there stands a screen with a curtain that is opened at various times during the Divine Liturgy, thus making the sanctuary visible but inaccessible to anyone but the sacred ministers. This sanctuary screen, or iconostasis, developed into an increasingly complex structure: numerous icons of saints and of the holy mysteries of the faith were mounted on it. While this screen appears to separate the divine world and the human world, it actually unites the two, symbolizing the reconciliation accomplished between the God of all and his creation.

An icon of the Savior, situated directly above the Royal Doors through which the priest brings Holy Communion to the congregation, holds the central place in the iconostasis. Icons of the Virgin Mother, representing the New Testament, and of John the Baptist, the last of the Old Testament prophets, take their place on either side of the Christ icon, forming what is called the Deisis prayer group. They stand in an attitude of prayer, indicating continual intercession for man who stands ever in need of the Lord's redeeming mercy. In time, other figures were ranked in this group, e.g., Saints Peter and Paul and the Archangels Gabriel and Michael. The general movement of the group is one of prayerful supplication before the enthroned Lord.

With time the tiers on the iconostasis grew in number; as this happened the top row came to hold representations of the Old Testament patriarchs. Below this was the row with the prophets, holding in their hands scrolls that contained the prophecies concerning the incarnation of the God-Man. At the center of the line of prophets came the icon of our Lady of the Sign, an image of the fulfillment of all these prophecies. Below the line of prophets came the tier holding the festal icons corresponding to the major feasts of the Church year: the Nativity of Christ, the Presentation in the temple, the Baptism of Jesus, the Transfiguration, the elevation of the Cross, the entry into Jerusalem, the Ascension and Pentecost; the birth of the Holy Virgin, her entry into the temple, the Annunciation, and the Assumption. In the whole ensemble the Feast of feasts holds a privileged place, the Resurrection of the Lord.

The entire iconostasis comes to its perfect center in the Royal Doors, symbolic of entrance into the kingdom of God. The lower tier, in which the Royal Doors are placed, is called the worship tier. Here the local icons are displayed: for example, the icon of the saint for whom the church is named, icons of the movable feasts and the current holy day. The icon of a movable feast remained on the iconostasis during a post-festal period, after which there was a celebration of its leave-taking. It is to the icons of this tier that the faithful paid their veneration most conveniently by reason of its position nearer the floor of the church. The devout expressed intimate communion with the saints represented there by placing a kiss on the faces of the icons and by burning candles before them.

Some of the icons painted on the iconostasis were very large. As private chapels became more common, artists painted smaller icons for them; even smaller ones were done for the homes of individuals who could afford them. Eventually every dwelling, from the palace of the richest prince to the hovel of the lowliest peasant, was adorned with its own icons. In the home a special corner of the living room was reserved for the icons. It was called the fair corner or the red corner since the word for red in Old Slavonic is the same as the word for beautiful. A lamp always burned before the icons. Placed in the central room of the home, the sacred images ensured divine protection for the family. Sometimes in the homes of the very wealthy, a separate room, called the room of the Cross, was filled with icons.

Upon entering his own home or that of another, the devout believer venerated the icons and only then greeted the people who were present. If he found no icons there, he asked whether God dwelt in that home or not. The Russian proverb, "Before committing an ugly deed, carry out the saints," indicates how unthinkable it was to be cruel or disrespectful in any way in the presence of an icon. Frequently families took an icon from their home to the church and before it made their special supplications.

The ancestral icon, a concrete symbol of the paternal blessing and the continuity of religious tradition, was the spiritual link between generations of Russian families. As a young couple began their own home and family, the ancestral icon, called the "paternal blessing," went with them. A very special example of an icon handed from generation to generation is the Vladimir Mother of God, the first illustration in this book. The new bride took this icon to her new home where it was placed in a corner of the bedroom. There it formed, as it were, the cornerstone of the new family. Under this Mother's loving care, each child of the family was conceived and born.

The family customs of the Russians, the rituals that were woven into their daily lives, the solemnity surrounding life's more important moments—all these were influenced by the rites and prayers of the Church. Celebrations great and small had as their background the unparalleled Easter glory, the radiance of transfiguration shown forth by this greatest of mysteries, illuminating the heart of man in his ordinary life. Keeping in mind the deep veneration of the Russians for their icons, we will now look closely at some festal icons and their place and meaning in the life of the faithful.

Chapter 4

The Annunciation

"**B**ehold, a virgin shall conceive and bear a son, and shall call his name Emmanuel." Isaias' prophecy (7:14) finds its fulfillment in the mystery represented by this icon, the annunciation, one of the favorite subjects of early Christian art. Early Christian writers likewise spoke of this event. Justin Martyr, living in the second century, in his "Dialogue" (#100) contrasts Mary and Eve:

> For Eve, who was a virgin and undefiled, having conceived the word of the serpent, brought forth disobedience and death. But the Virgin Mary received faith and joy when the Angel Gabriel announced the good tidings to her that the spirit of the Lord would come upon her, and the power of the Most High would overshadow her.[20]

In her *Hymns to the Church,* Gertrud von Le Fort expresses poetically what the icon communicates visually:

Rejoice, Mary Virgin, daughter of
    my earth, sister of my soul,
    rejoice, O joy of my joy!
I am as one who wanders
    through the night,
    but you are a house under stars.
I am a thirsty cup, but you are God's
    open sea.
Rejoice, Mary Virgin, blessed are those
    who call you blessed,
    never more shall child of man lose
    hope.[21]

The joy of all the Old Testament promises comes through what C.S. Lewis called "the Grand Miracle."[22] We see this joy expressed in the coloring of the icon, in the ornamentation on the buildings, in the posture of the messenger Gabriel, and in the swiftness of movement suggested by the flow of his garments. In most icons of the feast, Gabriel is pictured as though he were still in flight; although his feet are on the ground, one wing is raised,[23] a symbol, together with the staff, of his role as messenger.

In some icons the Mother is shown seated, a sign of her preeminent dignity and exaltation above the angels; in others she is standing as though poised to carry out the King's command to her. In Great Vespers for the feast of the Annunciation the Church recalls that the "Mother of God heard expressions she did not understand when the Archangel said to her the word of the Annunciation." It is with great restraint and reservation, through the quiet gestures of the Virgin, that the icon presents this event, the decisive moment in the world's history that was to decide its future fate. According to the choice of the iconographer, an icon of the annunciation depicts one of three moments: Mary turns in fear. She appears to question the dilemma of the message, and she lowers her head in submission to the call.

The appearance of and greeting by the angel in the first moment causes the Virgin distress, an appropriate response from one who immediately recognized and believed the angel to be sent by God. His intervention was completely unexpected, a sudden shock to the humble Virgin; thus she turns away in surprise, dropping the spindle of yarn that she was winding.

Sometimes Mary is shown in a mood of deep perplexity at the message. Recalling the laws of nature and remembering the fall of Eve, the Virgin is prudent, not accepting without question the extraordinary tidings from another world. Her hand is held, palm outward, as though warding off for the moment the unusual message, "How can this be?"

To show her moment of consent some iconographers depict the Virgin bowing her head and holding her hand to her heart. She accepts the great obedience that decided the fate of a world in need of a redeemer and savior.

All these moments combine in some icons. Leonid Ouspensky judges that the best tradition of icons for this feast shows

> the eyes of the Mother of God and the Archangel turned not towards one another but upwards, where we see the traditional portion of a sphere, the symbol of the high heavens, and rays issuing from it—the action of the Holy Spirit. The directions in which the Mother of God and the Archangel are looking meet in these descending rays. In this detail the fundamental meaning of the event is deeply felt and transmitted, namely, the unity of action and will, of God and his creature. . . . For the incarnation is not only an act of God's will, but also of the free will and faith of the Holy Virgin Mary (pp.173-4).

In her submission Mary replies, not to the messenger himself, but to the one who sent the message. This is noticeable in the upward position of her face. Her consent is not passive acceptance but rather a wholehearted, active surrender to God and his will for her and for the world. The mystery of the feast brings to our prayerful attention and contemplation the Virgin's full and association participation in the work of salvation. It is as though she demonstrates, in the name of all creatures, this voluntary cooperation with the Lord God.

Chapter 5

The Nativity, the Feast of Re-creation

Christ's coming among us is an historical event graciously willed by the Father as the path to our re-birth, the transfiguration of all mankind and the entire world of created things. In the nativity, the Eastern Church celebrates the renewal, sanctification, and re-creation of the whole universe. In a collect-hymn of the Divine Liturgy the Church sings:

> The Virgin today brings forth the Transubstantial, and the earth offers a cave to the Unapproachable. Angels give glory with shepherds, and the wise men journey with the star; because for our sake is born, as a little Child, God the Eternal.

In the nativity icon we see two fundamental aspects of the great mystery: first, the historical reality of the event in the world of time, showing in its details the humanity of God-with-us; second, the consequences of this event in our created world, reconciling all things in heaven and on earth in Christ.

Let us first look at the second aspect of the mystery. All of creation waits for the full redemption of the sons of God, the participation in the glorious freedom these sons are called to possess. The call that man holds to participate in the redemption of creation summons him with urgency to be renewed by the love of God made manifest in Christ Jesus. Creation has as its final purpose, as does man, ultimate transfiguration. In this icon of the nativity we see all creation taking part in the event, with representatives rendering each his own fitting homage and thanks:

> What shall we bring to thee, O Christ, when thou art born on earth as Man for our sake? For each of the creatures, who have their being from thee, brings thanks to thee: angels their songs, the heavens a star, the wise men gifts, the shepherds wonder, the earth a cave, the wilderness a manger, but we—the Virgin Mother.

"Through the tender mercy of our God" the day from on high dawns upon us "to give light to those who sit in darkness and in the shadow of death" (Luke 1:78f). Central to the composition of the icon is the yawning black mouth of the cave, symbolizing this world plunged into the darkness of sin through man's fall:

> The darkness of the cave is a rich symbol. It makes us think of that night outside time, the eternal mysterious night of the generation of the Word by the unbegotten Father: "When all things were in perfect silence and the night had come to the middle of her rapid course, thy Almighty Word leapt down from the highest heaven, from thy royal throne" (Wis. 18:14-15). The darkness of night in the Christmas icon turns our thoughts first of all to the illumination which the Lord's incarnation has brought us, an illumination which is the "light" of the sacred image.[24]

The wilderness which gave a place to the Sun of justice and truth is a fulfillment of the Old Testament prefiguration of the wilderness where the manna was given to the Israelites; the God who rained food upon them himself became man's food in the Eucharist. The Lamb slain for the sustenance of mankind on his journey to the Promised Land is laid upon the altar symbolized by the manger brought as a gift of the wilderness to the divine Word who became a baby to redeem mankind.

The emptying—*kenosis*—of the Godhead, his complete abasement, is shown by the swaddling clothes, the cave, the manger. The God invisible in nature becomes flesh for the sight and touch of man, for the healing of him whose life was fractured in the original fall. The swaddling clothes in which the Virgin wraps the Child point to the winding sheet in another cave, the sepulcher, to follow at the end of his abbreviated life among us.

> The inviolate body of the Virgin prefigured the inviolate tomb. The Lord came forth from both, preserving the seals intact.[25]

"The ox knows its owner, and the ass its master's crib; but Israel does not know, my people does not understand" (Is. 1:3). Although the Synoptics do not mention these attendants at the birth, the ox and ass stand immediately beside the Child in all icons of the nativity, at its very center; they have been faithful companions down through the centuries.

> To understand why the animals are in the picture, we must look at them with the eye of the believer and keep our ear open to the poetry of the Christian message. The animals, the manger—what have these to tell us if we would listen with the poet's ear? We too have an animal nature; we should understand the ox and ass. They speak innocence. They accept their master. They are not proud and haughty. Man's rebellious pride, in fact, is in his intellect, not in his animal body. The domestic animal may be intractable at times and may have to be treated firmly. But he has a true, if rudimentary devotion to his master, and a genuine desire to please him. Nothing could picture this more graphically than the image of the two animal heads looking in wonder at the helpless, bound-up infant who is their master. . . . They are not important for their physical bulk, but for their awesome expression of the animal nature which Christ undertook for our sakes.[26]

In a fourteenth-century mystery play entitled *Hail, Blessed Flower!*, we read this dialogue of Joseph and Mary regarding the attending animals at the scene of the nativity:

> Joseph: O Marie! Behold these beasts mild
> that make loving in their manner
> as they were men. . . .
> Mary: Their Lord . . .
> they worship him with might and main;
> the weather is cold as ye may feel—

to hold him warm they are full fain
  with their warm breath,
and breathe on him, has naught
    to lay on
  to warm him with.
O! now sleep my son, blest may
  he be.
And lie full warm these beasts
  between.[27]

The God of heaven and earth poised between
dumb beasts, wrapped in the poverty of *kenosis*—
this mystery far exceeds what any human mind
can conceive. Gertrud von Le Fort draws in
poetic lines the mystery we contemplate here in
the icon:

He who is strong has become tender,
  the Infinite has become small,
His power now is kindness,
  the Exalted has put on humility.
He finds room in the chamber of a maiden:
  His throne will be on her lap—
a cradle song will be enough praise
  for Him. . . .
Hail to her who carried the Lord!
             ("Advent," p. 39)

Eve became the mother of all the living; in the
new Eve we have the Mother of all the
redeemed. The Virgin Mother is the highest
thanksgiving offering that mankind could make
to the Creator, and in that Virgin mankind
affirms the salvation that is to come by means of
the incarnation of the very Person of God, the
Word. We celebrate in this feast the re-creation
of all things, the renewal of all who are born on
earth, renewal through this new Eve. Mary's
central position in the icons of this feast, as well
as her size, points out this unique role. She is
immediately beside the Child, yet outside the
cave; for she by a divine decree never dwelt in
the dark regions of sin. The position of the
Mother of God in the nativity is significant and
generally filled with dogmatic meaning, sometimes emphasizing the divine nature of the
Child, sometimes pointing to his human nature.

At the time of the Nestorian heresy, in order
to point up the *divine* origin of the Child and the
virginity of his Mother, the Virgin is half-
sitting, a sign of the absence of the usual
sufferings of childbearing. In the majority of
icons, however, so as to divest the incarnation of
all suspicion of illusion, the Mother is lying
down in weariness, reminding us of the *human*
nature of the Son. In some icons the Mother is
looking at the Child, cherishing in her heart all
the things that were said about him. In others
she is looking straight ahead at the world
outside.

In still others she looks with compassion on
Joseph, who is not part of the central group. He
is not the father and the icons usually show him
apart from the Mother-Child group. Joseph sits
at the lower edge of the icon, dismal and
confused. His state of doubt and turmoil is given
artistic expression by means of his hand resting
in perplexity on his cheek. Before him stands a
tempter in the guise of an old shepherd who tells
Joseph that a virgin birth is not possible; this
same objection has occurred throughout history
as the basis of numerous heresies, appearing in
different forms. Joseph's struggle with the
wonder of the virgin birth indicates not only his
own drama but that of all mankind in the
acceptance of that miracle which exceeds all
words and reason, the birth-giving of the Virgin
Mother to the Word of God.

Balancing the turmoil of Joseph is the faith
and belief of the Magi who approach either on
foot or on horseback bringing their gifts to the
Child. Rays of light from a star point out to them
the cave, rays that emanate from part of a
sphere that goes beyond the limits of the
picture, representing the heavenly world. Thus
the star is not simply a cosmic wonder but a
messenger from the world above telling of the
birth of him who formed the stars. The Magi
represent the beginning of the nations, the
adoration of the heathen world. They are
learned men who have come on a long journey
"from the knowledge of what is relative to the
knowledge of what is absolute" (Ouspensky, p.
160). The coming of the Magi holds two main
lessons in the festival of re-creation, the first of
which is that the Church accepts and elevates
all human science,

provided that the relative light of the
extra-Christian revelation brings those
who serve it to the worship of the absolute
light (Ouspensky, p. 160).

The Magi are of different ages to show that
knowledge of God and his revelation are granted
to men independently of their age and worldly
experience.

Your birth, O Christ our God, shed on the
world the light of wisdom, for they that
had served the stars were taught by a star

to worship You, the Sun of Holiness, and to know You, the Dawn from on high. Glory to You, O Lord!

At the nativity angels performed a two-fold role: that of messengers of the glad tidings and that of adorers glorifying God for this marvel. Some angels are turned heavenward, some are bent toward earth, bearing the news to the shepherds and, in these men, to all mankind.

The shepherds are the first of the Israelite people to worship the Lord. They are simple, unsophisticated men who hear the message from the heavenly world in the midst of their daily work.

Truly the Lord is the Sun of all wisdom. "He is a kingdom in the hearts of men."[28] Just as in the Book of Numbers (17:8) the rod of Aaron came to bud and blossom in the night, so the Virgin Mary miraculously gave us the most blessed Jesus Christ who brought and ever continues to bring new life and beauty and fragrance to a world that awaits his full revealing in the sons he has fashioned after his own image.

> Come and see
> The cause why things thus fragrant be.
> 'Tis He is born whose quickening birth
> Gives life and luster, public mirth,
> To Heaven, and the under-Earth.
> Chor.   We see Him come,
>   and know Him ours,
>   Who with His sunshine
>   and His showers
>   Turns all the patient ground
>   to flowers.[29]

Chapter 6

The Presentation of Christ in the Temple, the "Meeting"

Anna, the mother of the boy Samuel, took her first-born and only son to the temple, there to offer him to Yahweh through Heli (1 Sam. 1:24-28). In this event the Old Testament prefigures the offering of another Mother in the new dispensation, the Virgin Mary who brought her only Son to the temple to offer him according to the Law through Simeon who is honored as the host of God—*Theodokos* in Greek.

The feast of the Presentation of Christ in the temple, often called the "Meeting," is very ancient. A fourth-century pilgrim from Aquitania, Aetheria, whose diary is invaluable for its information concerning early feasts of the Church year, wrote that she saw the feast of the Presentation celebrated with great solemnity in Jerusalem. In Great Vespers of the feast the Church praises the Mother and Child as it celebrates the occasion when the Creator of the Law accomplishes what was laid down by the Law. To fulfill what was written in the Books of Exodus and Leviticus, the First-born of all creation is consecrated to God. The event as recorded in the second chapter of Luke's Gospel provides the basis of the liturgical texts and of the iconography of this feast.

Christ is not pictured in the swaddling clothes of the nativity but rather in a short vest-like garment. He sits on the arms of Simeon as on a throne, sometimes raising his hand in blessing. Among a group of icons called the Emmanuel-type, Christ is always shown as a young boy. This representation is used in the icons for the feast of the Presentation.

The Mother stands with her hands covered by a large veil or *maphorion*, the gesture used in icons to signify offering. The purification of Mary is almost forgotten in the icon and in the liturgy of the feast. The central stage is occupied by the meeting—*hypapante* in Greek—of the Child-Messiah with his people in the persons of Simeon and Anna. It is also a celebration of the meeting of the Old and New Testaments. Whereas the birth of Christ and the adoration of the shepherds and Magi were confined to the small circle of the Holy Family, this event shows Christ appearing in the midst of his people. Behind the Mother stands Joseph, his hands also covered, holding in his robe the two doves, symbolic of the united offering of Jews and Gentiles in the one Person of Christ as well as of the two Testaments of which Christ is the total fulfillment.

Anna sometimes stands near Mary, some-times behind Simeon. She holds a scroll which bears the words, "This Child is the creator of heaven and earth." With her head tilted back and her face lifted up, she realizes that this Child is the fulfillment of all her longings, the culmination of her many years of vigil in the temple of the Lord.

Simeon holds a place of great importance in the feast and in the icon. The "host of God" leans forward, holding the Child in both hands which are covered in veneration. "O Christ God, the Virgin's womb was made holy by your birth, and blessed were the arms of Simeon." Vladimir Lossky, commenting on this feast and its icon,

states that the liturgical texts exalt Simeon as

> the greatest of the prophets: more even than Moses, Simeon deserves the title of "He who has seen God" for to Moses God appeared enveloped in darkness, whilst Simeon carried in his arms the eternal incarnate Word (pp. 171-2).

People of the early Church tried to fathom who this Simeon might have been. Some tried to make the "just elder" into a priest of the temple; yet icons do not show him in priestly garb. His head is uncovered, he wears his hair unshorn like that of a Nazarite, he is garbed in a robe that flows down to his bare feet. Others imagined him to be a doctor of the Law, the son of Hillel, and the father of Gamaliel, the teacher of St. Paul. Others yet fancied him to be one of seventy translators of the Bible, whom God had preserved in life for 350 years until the Messiah should come upon earth. Whoever he might have been, he is the revealer to the nations of the Light, Christ. Through his prophetic utterance to the Mother of God, he is also the one who revealed the Cross.

> And while Simeon was holding Life in Person, he asked him to be delivered of his own present life and said: "Dismiss me now, O Master, that I may tell Adam how my eyes have seen the Eternal God made man without undergoing change, and bringing about the salvation of the world. . . . my eyes have seen you, Eternal Light, God the Savior of the people called Christians."

Whereas iconographers worked according to patterns of rather strict conventions, nevertheless their creative powers gave individual expression to the canonical models they followed. In the icon of the presentation we find a beautiful freedom of expression, an intimacy and warmth befitting the mystery of the Dawn's appearance from on high to make known the tender mercy of our God.

Chapter 7

The Baptism, the Theophany

" . . . the grace of God has appeared for the salvation of all men" (Titus 2:11). The baptism of Christ is the manifestation, the theophany, of him who sanctified the waters of the Jordan that man might be freed from sin. In a discourse on the baptism of the Lord, quoted by Ouspensky (p. 167), St. John Chrysostom says:

> It is not the day when Christ was born that should be called Epiphany, but the day when he was baptized. Not through his birth did he become known to all, but through his baptism. Before the day of baptism he was not known to the people.

The baptism of Christ has two aspects: on this day was revealed the truth that there are three Persons in one God and on this day the ritual ablutions established by the prophets were brought to their perfection for upon them Christ founded the New Testament sacrament of baptism.

The revelation of the Trinity was made manifest in plain forms accessible to the senses. The baptizer John heard the voice of the Father. He saw the Holy Spirit in the form of a dove. Both gave testimony to the

Son of God in the person of the baptized. These words are on the lips of the faithful in the celebration of this feast:

> Our God, the Trinity, has this day revealed himself to us indivisibly; for the Father bore witness to his parenthood with manifest testimony, the Spirit descended from the heavens like a dove, and the Son bowed his most pure head to the Forerunner and was baptized.

There is an analogy between the appearance of the dove at this event and the dove at the time of the flood: the dove, bearing an olive branch of peace and tranquillity to Noe's ark, brought the message that the world had been purified of its iniquities and had returned to peace; the Spirit, descending in the form of a dove, bears the message of the remission of our sins through the tender mercy of our God.

Christ is shown standing against a background of water as though he were in a cave, the iconographer's way of indicating that he is submerged and surrounded by water. This shows that he has taken upon himself the sins of the world. He is covered with the waters of the Jordan in order to purify the water for our renewal and purification. The Savior blesses the waters that cover him, thus by his immersion making them holy. It is Christ who comes to John to be baptized. It is through his own initiative as master that he draws near the servant for this ministration. The waters from then on become an image, not of death, but of rebirth, of new life.[30] This same Christ will later descend, unharmed, into the waters of death, defeating once for all in his own victory the death and sin of all mankind.

The nakedness of Christ emphasizes the emptying, the *kenosis,* of his Godhead. By this nakedness he clothed the nakedness of Adam and that of all mankind with the new garment of immortality and glory. The angels stand as servants, their cloaks covering their hands.[31] In later icons angels are sometimes shown holding garments with which to clothe Christ on his emergence from the waters.

In many representations of Jesus' baptism two figures are at the feet of Christ as he stands in the Jordan. One of them is a male figure turning his back to Christ. This is an allegorical representation of the waters of the Jordan which, as Psalm 113 expresses it, "turned back" to let the Israelites cross over. The other is a female figure, sometimes shown running away. She represents the Red Sea which looked and fled, making a safe path for the Chosen People and prefiguring the sure way afforded by the waters of baptism for entry into the kingdom of God.

On the feast of the Baptism the faithful of the Eastern Church celebrate the blessing of water to be used when the priest sprinkles their homes. In the blessing of the homes, he prays:

> O Lord, be in our thoughts, in our words, in our deeds, in our tears, and in our laughter. O Lord, let your presence be felt in this house, and in those who enter therein, as it was felt by John as you were baptized in the Jordan River.

Isaias (12:3) promises that we shall draw water with joy from the springs of salvation, for, in the words at the Communion during the Divine Liturgy, "the Lord is God and has appeared to us."

Chapter 8

The Transfiguration

The nativity and the baptism show Christ in his *kenosis* as a servant come to clothe mankind and all creation with robes of future transformation and incorruptibility. The transfiguration shows us Jesus "in the form of God" (Phil. 2:6). Here again we have a theophany of the Trinity.

The transfiguration is prefigured, though vaguely, in the Old Testament by the Feast of Tabernacles. The people dwelt in huts for seven days, recalling God's protection while they wandered in the desert. Thus Peter desired to dwell on the mount of glory in tents which he offered to build. Easter celebrates the beginning of the grain harvest, Pentecost, its finale. The reaping of the final crop symbolizes transfiguration.

Most of the icons of this feast follow the account according to St. Matthew. The apostles fall flat upon hearing the voice of the Father and upon seeing the dazzling bright light. They appear dazed, lost in ecstasy at the overwhelming revelation of the Godhead. Their amazement suggests in artistic terms the uncreated character of the light. The transfigured Christ in brilliant garments stands before a many-pointed star inscribed on the *mandorla*, the circle or oval used in iconography as a symbol of heaven, divine glory. In one of the collect-hymns the Church sings that on this occasion Peter, James, and John received "as much of [God's] glory as they could hold" so that

> when they saw you crucified, they might know that you suffered willingly, and might proclaim you to the world as being the true radiance of the Father.

In the ninth chapter of the Gospel according to Luke, we find Jesus revealing to his disciples that he must suffer many things, including rejection and death, before he would be raised on the third day (Luke 9:22f). Prior to that time, at the beginning of his public life, Jesus himself had undergone the temptation of the desert. Dame Aemiliana Lohr writes of temptation, specifically of Christ's temptation before his public life and his suffering and death:

> Temptation stands at the beginning of the way of pain, and surrounds its continuance. It seeks to draw the soul away from the saving Passion. . . . The essence of temptation is the desire to make shortcuts on the way, to come of one's own power to glory and to despise the appointed hours; to go round the Cross. . . the temptation of Christ was . . . an untimely and self-willed revelation of the glory of God which was his. . . . To strengthen the faith of his apostles for the time of the Passion, the glory of the resurrection is anticipated for them to see for a moment on the mountain. . . . The Lord unveils, far from the crowd, his true essence, in order to give them the certainty of the undying life which no earthly death can influence. Because they believe, their belief is to be strengthened by vision; but what they see will remain for them to be silent about , for the Lord wills to test the faith of the others first with his humble humanity. Only he who believes in the Son of Man is worthy to see God among men.[32]

The figures of Moses and Elias outline the Christ whose garments are shining white, a fact which receives in Mark 9:3 more attention than the brilliance of his face—no laundry on earth could make his garments so white! St. John Chrysostom explains the reason for the presence of Moses, holding the tables of the Law, and of Elias, an elderly man standing at Christ's left in a posture of supplication. They stand for the Law and the prophets. Each had been given a vision of God, Moses on Sinai and Elias on Carmel. Moses signifies the dead and Elias the living for he was taken up into heaven in a fiery chariot (cf. 2 Kings 2). On an icon of the sixteenth or seventeenth century, an angel is depicted as drawing Moses out of the tomb of death while another angel leads Elias from a cloud. God is Lord of the living and the dead; he appears in the glory of the transfiguration with the promise of future glory for all.

This feast of the Transfiguration shows us not only the revelation of the Godhead but also the deification of man, the glory that is in store for him. We have already spoken of this truth as one of the doctrines underlying Russian iconography. Let us now turn our reflection to this aspect of the mystery.

Through the coming of Jesus among us, we are empowered to become images, icons of him. Occasionally through history saints of both East and West have been transfigured with light in a fashion comparable to that brightness of Christ himself on Mount Tabor. Some holy writers speak of this experience of divine light. Teresa of Avila, Francis and Clare of Assisi, Catherine of Bologna, Catherine of Genoa, to name only a few, are saints of the West who have been immersed in such bodily glorification at times during their lives. What is the meaning of such glorification? Kallistos Timothy Ware in an essay "The Transfiguration of the Body" in *Sacrament and Image* considers this question:

> First, the transfiguration—whether of Christ or of Christ's saints—underlines the significance of the human body for Christian theology. When Christ was transfigured on Mount Tabor, his divine glory was manifested in and through his human body: through their physical eyes the disciples saw that "in him all the fullness of the Godhead dwells bodily" (Col. 2:9). And just as Christ's glory is not only inward but physical and bodily, so it is with that of the saints: their transfiguration emphasises that man's sanctification . . . is not something that concerns the soul alone, but something that involves the body (Ware, p. 21).

The burdens of this life, the ills of the human body, the evil desires that plague us are specific consequences of man's original fall. Since that time the body has existed with a leaning toward sin, that is, not in its natural condition as God had created it. The transfiguration of Christ and his saints in their bodily life shows us, therefore, the body as God made it, what our human nature would be now but for the fall of Adam, as well as what our human nature is called to be. A text from Great Vespers for the feast reads:

> Transfigured today on Mount Tabor in his disciples' presence, Christ revealed the original beauty of the image, assuming man's substance into himself. . . . Transfigured, thou hast made Adam's nature, which was grown dim, to shine once more as lightning, transforming it into the glory and splendor of thy Godhead.

Some of the saints, as we have intimated, attain even in this present life a degree of incorruptibility that was man's at the beginning of time and which he will possess after the resurrection of the body. Also the bodies of some saints are preserved from the usual corruption of death.

> . . . the transfiguration—whether of Christ or of Christ's saints—is an eschatological event, a foretaste and anticipation of the parousia. The bodily glorification of the saints illustrates the position of the Christian "in the world but not of it"— placed at a point of intersection between this present age and the age to come, and living in both ages at once. The last times are not merely an event in the future, but have already begun (p. 21).

Kallistos Ware then asks why it is that if the body is deified together with the soul so few saints experience incorruptibility and outward glorification:

> Only once during his earthly life, and then only for a short time, did Jesus appear transfigured by the divine light. . . . by a deliberate act of self-emptying he concealed this glory on other occasions; and it is only at the second coming, when he shall appear again in power and great majesty, that men will see his human body as it really is, in its full wonder. So it is with the saints. During this earthly life their true glory is nearly always concealed, only being made physically manifest in a few cases and on rare occasions. But when the dead rise again at the Last Day, the saints will be revealed as they truly are, deified both in soul and in body. . . . The homilies of Macarius (late fourth—early fifth century) speak at length of man's future transfiguration at the resurrection of the body. . . . "At the day of resurrection the glory of the Holy Spirit *comes out from within*, decking and covering the bodies of the saints—the glory which they had before, but hidden within their souls. What a man has now, the same then comes forth externally in the body. . . ." It is this transfigured "resurrection body," resplendent with the light of the Holy Spirit, that the icon painter attempts symbolically to depict (pp. 29-30).

The whole of material creation is called to participate in this transfiguration of man, the full revelation of the sons of God.

The profound beauty of an icon is gentle. It does not force its way; it does not intrude. It asks for patience with the uneasiness of early acquaintance. It asks for time spent before it in stillness of gazing. More important, it asks the one praying to allow himself to be gazed upon by it. One must yield space within himself to the icon and its persistent beauty. An icon is prayer and contemplation transformed into art. When exquisite art combines with prayer to become a work of worship and wonder, the art becomes sacramental. It manifests to us the God who breaks through all signs and symbols with truth.

Our Lady of Vladimir
12th Century Byzantine or 13th Century
  Russian Copy
Plate 1

Tretyakov State Gallery
Moscow

The Savior

Early 15th Century
Andrei Rublev
Plate 2

Tretyakov State Gallery
Moscow

The Nativity

14th to 15th Century
Novgorod School
Plate 4

Tretyakov State Gallery
Moscow

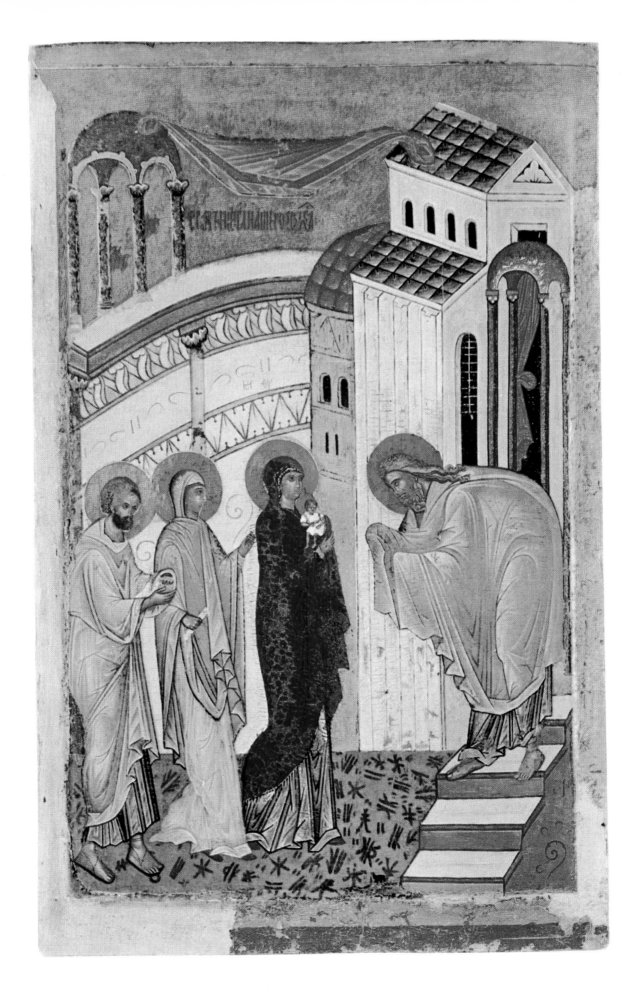

The Baptism, the Theophany

17th Century
Ukrainian School

Plate 6

Ukrainian State Museum
Kiev

The Transfiguration

Early 15th Century
Novgorod School
Plate 7

Collection Korin
Moscow

The Raising of Lazarus

15th Century
Novgorod School

Plate 8

Russian State Museum
Leningrad

The Entry into Jerusalem

Early 15th Century
Andrei Rublev Period
Plate 9

Annunciation Cathedral
Moscow Kremlin

The Last Supper

11th Century
Novgorod School
Plate 10

State Museum for Russian Art
Kiev

The Descent from the Cross

15th Century
Attributed to North Russian School
Plate 12

Tretyakov State Gallery
Moscow

The Holy Trinity
Early 15th Century
Andrei Rublev
Plate 16
Tretyakov State Gallery
Moscow

Chapter 9

The Raising of Lazarus

The Books of Kings relate the stories of Elias and Eliseus. Among their mighty deeds are parallel accounts of each raising a boy from death to life and restoring him to his mother. The holy prophets prefigure Christ. The resurrection of the two sons foreshadows the mercy shown to the dead Lazarus whom Jesus raised to life after four days and restored, in full view of the people, to his two sisters Mary and Martha (John 11:1-46). In the icon of the raising of Lazarus, we see the city walls in the background. The people come out from the gates in tears. We sense in the picture a stress on movement, quick and decisive, as one man busies himself with taking the stone away from the entrance, while another has hold of one end of the winding sheet that wraps the standing Lazarus.

Christ extends his right hand in blessing. His left hand holds a scroll with the words of command, borne out by his very posture: "Lazarus, come forth!" Behind Christ are the apostles and at his feet are Mary and Martha prostrate in adoration. On some representations of this event, the friends surrounding Lazarus make known vividly the unpleasantness of the stench by covering nose and mouth with their robes. The Gospel account and the iconography of the event leave no doubts about its authenticity; all its details are reproduced. The care in the representation of detail indicates the importance of this sign, the last miracle Jesus performed before his Passion, death, and glorious rising.

Christ is on his way to voluntary death, the Christ who will conquer death through surrendering to it in his own body and who will afterwards be delivered from it by the Father. The raising of Lazarus takes place in the presence of the people, in contrast to the call to resurrection given by Jesus to the daughter of Jairus. The latter event was concealed, whereas the command to Lazarus went out like a clarion openly before the crowd. By this miracle Christ strengthens faith in his divine power and gives a vivid assurance of future resurrection for all. More immediately, he prepares his disciples to believe in his own glorious rising to be accomplished within a short time.

Jesus was aware of the illness of his friend Lazarus and yet did not go to work a healing. In fact, he delayed for several days after Lazarus' death, meanwhile giving his disciples lessons along the way about the light—lessons incomprehensible in the face of grave illness and death but understandable in the light shed by Lazarus' and Christ's resurrection.

The raising of Lazarus is closely connected with the glorious entry of Christ into the holy city, Jerusalem. On the day before Palm Sunday the Eastern Church celebrates the "Saturday of Lazarus." Some of the texts of the Divine Liturgy and the Hours serve for both feasts, such as this hymn:

> O Christ God, when you raised Lazarus from the dead, before the time of your Passion, you confirmed the future resurrection of all. We, too, like the children of old, carry before you the symbols of your triumph and victory and cry out to you, the Conqueror of Death: "Hosanna in the highest! Blessed is he who comes in the name of the Lord."

There are differences between the raising of Lazarus and Christ's resurrection. Of himself Lazarus could not come out of the clutches of death; Christ commanded those standing by to roll aside the stone. When Lazarus stands forth at the mouth of the cave of death, he is bound hand and foot in a cloth which others must loosen; he is powerless to free himself of his fetters. As far as we know, Lazarus was restored to the kind of life he had known four days previously; Christ's resurrection was to a more glorious form and mode of existence. C. S. Lewis in *Miracles* says:

> The fitness of the miracle lies in the fact that he who will raise all men at the general resurrection here does it small and close, and in an inferior—a merely anticipatory—fashion. For the mere restoration of Lazarus is as inferior in splendour to the glorious resurrection of the New Humanity as stone jars are to the green and growing vine or five little barley loaves to all the waving bronze and gold of a fat valley ripe for harvest.[33]

In this event of Christ's life we see clearly both his human and divine nature. He questions, "Where have you laid him?" He weeps with the mourning sisters and friends of Lazarus. And yet Christ had foreknowledge of the death and raising to life of Lazarus (John 11:11-15); in his omnipotence he reverses the course of decomposition. He reunites the body and soul of a man already four days in the hold of the enemy. In a few days this enemy will attempt ineffectually to destroy Life. Lazarus the man, the utterly poor man, man in sin, is an image of Adam crying out for redemption. Christ, the Vanquisher of death, breathes into creation the sweet smell of new life.

We have spoken above of the manner in which nature is portrayed in iconography. Certain conventions are used to show that the entire created world is meant to participate in man's future transfigured state. Rocks and hills, for example, are painted in very unnatural shapes. In this icon and in some of the other prints included in this book, we see the glee with which the Russian painters depicted mountains. Large areas of Russia are endlessly flat; artists living in these areas might never have seen real hills, yet they would have heard about them in travelers' tales and seen them in Byzantine paintings. The mountains here have grotesque shapes. With all of creation they await the full redemption of the sons of God.

Chapter 10

The Entry into Jerusalem

The icon of Christ's triumphal entry into the city which will soon cast him outside its walls is regal in character and gives a preview of Easter joy. The immediate occasion for the public acclamation that accompanied Christ into Jerusalem was the raising of Lazarus from the dead. Whereas the chief priests and the Pharisees were disturbed about the many signs and marvels of Jesus and sought to take his life, many of the people who were at the grave of Lazarus saw and believed. It is the latter who made great festivity at Jesus' entrance into Jerusalem, welcoming him with the honors given to conquerors and to persons of high rank in recognition of their valor.

The scene is directly outside the city walls. The background is very similar to the one of the previous icon, the raising of Lazarus. Since donkeys were uncommon in Russia, many icons show Christ riding a horse. He gives a blessing as he passes. The apostles are to his left and the Hebrew crowds come from the gates of the city, carrying their children in their arms or on their shoulders and holding palm branches in their hands.

Children are not mentioned in the Gospel account of this event but tradition gives them an important and unique role—this is emphasized both by the iconography and by the Divine Liturgy and the Hours. Except rarely, it is children who are portrayed as spreading garments on the path. It is children, too, who clamber up the tree overhead to cut the branches and toss them down to be strewn on the way of the King. The gladness of the children held no ulterior motives, no plots of earthly power or gain. They stand in contrast to the rejoicing crowd who expected that the Messiah would finally make known his earthly power; the crowd looked to him to establish on firm ground the kingdom of Israel and to annihilate Israel's enemies. When they were disappointed in their hopes, they renounced what Christ was offering them and changed their cries from "Hosanna!" to "Crucify him!"

Christ reverses all their hopes in a reckless paradox: what appeared to be submission to the enemy death would be the very conquest of that enemy. The power of the Messiah would establish itself in terms made known by Christ himself: "Take my yoke upon you, and learn from me; for I am gentle and lowly in heart, and you will find rest for your souls. For my yoke is easy and my burden is light" (Matthew 11:29f). What an incomprehensible message from the mouth of a king and conqueror! John the Evangelist tells us that Jesus' own disciples "did not understand this at first; but when Jesus was glorified, then they remembered" (John 12:16).

Jerusalem is the image of the blessed kingdom of God. In the blessing of the palms on this feast of Christ's entry into the city, the priest prays for the attainment of this kingdom:

> And like unto those multitudes and children who offered unto thee Hosanna may we also in hymns and spiritual songs, attain unto the life-giving resurrection on the third day, through the same Christ Jesus our Lord; with whom thou art blessed, together with thine all-holy, and good, and life-giving Spirit, now, and ever, and unto ages of ages. Amen.

Chapter 11

The Holy Supper

The office of Matins for Great Thursday speaks of the event portrayed on this icon, the Holy Supper, and its significance:

> He who is the Lord of all and God the Creator, the Passionless One, united the creature with himself, in that he did humble himself; and himself becoming the Passover, did offer himself in anticipation unto those on behalf of whom it was his will to die, crying, "Eat ye my Body, and ye shall be strengthened in faith."

This icon shows Christ at the table with the apostles. The figure of the betrayer Judas is surrounded in some icons with a dark nimbus or halo; in others he is pictured with a demon entering his mouth. He stretches his hand toward the dish. Icons of the Holy Supper refer visually, in many instances, to the words of Christ, "Truly, truly, I say to you, one of you will betray me" (John 13:21). We see the consternation that followed these words in the expressions on the faces of the friends with whom he shared this meal.

The Divine Liturgy and the Hours for this day emphasize the traitor Judas and his black deed. In a hymn for Great Thursday we hear Judas called the one who is

> ailing with covetousness . . . sick with the love of silver. . . . All you who love riches, think and meditate on the man who hung himself for this very love.

And in each celebration of the Divine Liturgy the priest says this prayer before Communion:

> Of thy Mystical Supper, O Son of God, accept me today as a communicant; for I will not speak of thy Mystery to thine enemies, neither like Judas will I give thee a kiss, but like the thief will I confess thee: Remember me, O Lord, in thy Kingdom.

An icon of Christ washing the feet of the disciples after the Holy Supper shows all the twelve apostles, including Judas. A verse in the Matins of the day recalls the washing:

> The apostles, united in the bond of love, having dedicated themselves unto Christ who reigns over all, made beautiful their feet by going and proclaiming the glad tidings of peace unto all the world.

Judas is a dismal exception to the quiet flow of harmony and peace in this verse. On the same icon of the washing we see, by contrast, Peter's typical zest and devotion to the Master. As Christ washes his feet, Peter holds his garment out of the way with one hand; with the other he points to his head, "Lord, not my feet only but also my hands and my head."

Let us continue our reflections on the icon of the Holy Supper. It is this icon that holds a central place in the iconostasis or the altar screen, just over the Royal Doors at the entrance to the Holy of Holies. Directly underneath it the clergy distribute Communion to the faithful saying:

> The servant of God, N., receives the precious and holy Body and Blood of our Lord and God and Savior, Jesus Christ, unto the remission of his sins, and unto life everlasting.

The practice of the reception of the Eucharist among Eastern rite Christians differs from the practice in the West. While frequent and even daily Communion is not uncommon in the Latin rite, in the Eastern Churches the Divine Liturgy itself is offered according to a different rhythmic pattern on several days of the week, perhaps, but not daily.

The sacrament of the Eucharist makes possible the actual entrance of the Church into the kingdom of God; it is *the* sacrament of the kingdom, with all other sacraments relating to it as to their heart. From the early Fathers of the Church we learn that one receives the water of baptism in order that he might feed on the heavenly food of the Eucharist. In this great mystery we see Christ holding himself in his own hands, a gesture of offering in which he wished to be remembered without end, desiring to feed poor and hungry man with his own divine life. In her poem "Corpus Christi Mysticum," Gertrud von Le Fort addresses the Church:

> He has found us in the lap
>   of our wretchedness
>   and has put on humility in our hands.
> He dwells in the wine of your chalices
>   and in the white bread of your altars,
> You lay Him on our longing,
>   you place Him on our hungering lips.
> You lay Him deeply into the heart
>   of our solitude,
>   and it opens like gates unbarred.

(p. 32).

Chapter 12

The Crucifixion

Basic to Christian piety is the Cross and loving adherence to all it represents. Each time a Christian makes the sign of the Cross, he manifests the power of God: "The word of the Cross is folly to those who are perishing, but to us who are being saved, it is the power of God" (1 Cor. 1:18). Any mourning that is present in iconographic portrayals of the Crucifixion is tempered by the certainty of hope conveyed in the bodily postures, the strong lines, and colors. It is as though the iconographer were trying to show the victory of Christ's "hour." Christ, in a conversation with Philip and Andrew, stated that his coming to his "hour" was for the glorification of his Father. That "hour" which had not yet come at the time of his first miracle at Cana is the turning point in history. With it a whole new beginning breaks through; this breakthrough is prepared for by a growing crescendo of signs and miracles, from Cana to the raising of Lazarus. The "hour" of the *Kyrios,* the most high Lord, is his own glorification which would include the seeming triumph of his enemies in his Passion and death, and finally his resurrection. In death he would overthrow forever the power of Satan, sin and death.

The iconographer seems to be stating pictorially that apart from the folly of the Cross there is no receiving the wisdom of God. The Cross stands as the great paradox of all times: it carries with loving arms God's Son, poured out in voluntary *kenosis*, in obedience to his Father, to whom belong the times and the hours and the seasons, in whom is found the answer to all puzzles. The divine nature of Christ undergoes no change in his Passion and death. He continues as God, the Word, the wisdom, and the power of God.

> I take the shoes from my feet,
>   I put off all that is finite and tread
>   on a land without borders. . . .
> Holy God, Holy Strength, Holy Immortal,
> Thou God under my sin,
>   Thou God under my weakness,
>   Thou God under my death.
> I lay my lips upon Thy wounds—
>   Lord, I lay my soul upon Thy cross
>   (von Le Fort, p. 46).

In many icons of the Crucifixion, Christ is shown still alive. By confronting the living Christ, the worshipper is drawn into direct communion with the One who died to save him. The victory over hell effected by the Cross is illustrated by the black pit at its base. In the cavern is the skull of Adam; recall how fond Paul and the very early Church were of contrasting the first Adam and Christ, the new Adam. To this day in Jerusalem the Greek Orthodox Church keeps an "Adam Chapel."

The walls of the city form the background of the icon. They have both historical and spiritual significance:

> . . . the bodies of those animals whose blood is brought into the sanctuary by the high priest as a sacrifice for sin are burned outside the camp. So Jesus also suffered outside the gate in order to sanctify the people through his own blood. Therefore let us go forth to him outside the camp, bearing abuse for him. For here we have no lasting city but we seek the city which is to come (Heb. 13:11-14).

Against the open sky and above the gates of the city, the upper part of the Cross with the arms of Christ extended signifies the cosmic meaning of his death, which has changed the entire universe.

The mourning that is shown in icons of the Crucifixion is balanced and restrained. For instance, Mary stands to the right of Christ, upright and steady. In some representations she seems to be calling the terrified John to contemplate with her the mystery of salvation that is taking place before their eyes. In some icons the youthful John looks as though he were hiding his eyes from the sight of what is happening. Holy women stand by the Virgin Mother. The centurion Longinus, standing behind John, looks up at Christ and acknowledges his divinity as he crosses himself in a gesture of repentance. Some icons have ministering angels and symbolic figures that represent the synagogue and the Church. The icon of Dionysius shows two angels at the left of Christ motioning away the synagogue and two angels on the right leading the way to the life-giving Cross.

As Christians we live in the certainty of the hope given by our dying Lord. The hope of being remembered by him, a hope had by the thief in his last hour, is voiced in a prayer of the Church:

> When the thief beheld the Author of Life hanging upon the Cross, he said: If thou who art crucified with us, were not God incarnate, the sun would not have hidden its rays, neither would the earth have quaked with trembling. But do thou who suffer all things, remember me in thy kingdom, Lord.

Chapter 13

The Descent from the Cross
and the Entombment

O n Friday of the "Silent Week" the descent from the Cross is commemorated, along with the entombment, in the Office of the Burial of Christ. It is marked with faith and hope. The time of Christ in the tomb is seen by Eastern Christians as a time of renewing and invigorating sleep that followed his strenuous sufferings.

The celebration of the morning Office of Good Friday, in practice often anticipated on Great Thursday evening, is characterized by twelve Gospel passages drawn from the four evangelists. These accounts tell the story of the arrest, the Passion, and the death of Jesus and are interspersed with poetic dirge-like compositions which echo the main theme of each passage. Here are some examples:

The most handsome of men is
   seen today without beauty!
The Lord Jesus Christ is
   laid today in the tomb
To give back to all men the splendor of God.

O Jesus, King and Master of all,
   well do we know
That you accepted this death
   for the life of us all.
Oh, the wonder,
   Oh, the divine condescension! . . .

You were like a grain of wheat
   in the bosom of the earth:
The grain died and the wheat
   sprang up a hundredfold.
In truth, you are mankind's Bread and Life.

The entombment of Christ is celebrated with a solemn procession. The dead Christ is depicted on a cloth called the *epitaphios*, which varies in ornateness from one church to another. Sometimes this cloth carries a representation of the entire scene of the descent from the Cross. Another form would be a portrayal of the dead Christ as he would appear in the tomb if one were gazing down at him. This representation is the object of great veneration by the faithful.

In the Office of the Burial, which takes place on Great Friday evening, the *epitaphios* is borne in procession from the Holy Table, out of the building, and around the entire structure. It is carried inside again and placed in a representation of the tomb usually set up in the center of the nave. In the celebration of this Office the priest assumes the role of Joseph of Arimathea who sought the body of Christ to give him a place of rest and repose.[34] This rest of Jesus in the tomb wakes mankind from the ponderous sleep of iniquity, as one of the eulogies of the Office proclaims:

Thou didst fall asleep in the grave,
   O Christ,
with sleep which is natural to creatures,
and from the heavy sleep of sin didst
   raise up the human race.

It is believed that the icons of the descent and the entombment are the only icons that portray death. The representation of the dormition, the assumption of the Virgin Mary, shows the Mother on her couch in death but the soul of the sinless Virgin is being taken up into heaven in the form of a small child. The portrayals of death in the two icons of the Lord's descent from the Cross and his entombment do not have an early Christian source other than Scripture.

Chapter 14

The Descent into Hades, the Harrowing of Hell

Christianity has no mystery more profound than that of Christ's resurrection. The resurrection gives completion to the truth of the incarnation and testifies to the divine personhood of Jesus. To preach Christianity meant, first and foremost, to preach the risen Lord; in early Christianity an apostle was one who had been an eyewitness of this Lord risen and now reigning at the right hand of the Father. *The* gospel, in fact, was the resurrection and its consequences; the four gospels were written only later, for the benefit of those who had already received and accepted *the* gospel. The resurrection is the central theme of every sermon of the apostles in the Book of Acts. At Athens the people had the idea that Paul was talking to them of *two* new gods: Jesus and *Anastasis*—the Greek word for "resurrection." Easter is

the "feast of feasts" and
> the celebration of celebrations; it excels all other festivals, as the sun excels the stars; and this is true not only of human and earthly feasts, but also of those belonging to Christ and celebrated in his honor.[35]

With this mystery the concept of re-creation brought out in the iconography of Christ's nativity comes to perfection. With the resurrection a whole new time period began. One of the dirges from the Office of the Burial of Christ points out that all creation made its response to the death of Jesus:

> At the time of your death,
>   the whole earth quaked with fear.
> At the time of your divine burial,
>   the sun hid its rays,
> for you, O Christ, are the Lord of Nature.

The Gospels are silent and give no details about the actual moment of Christ's resurrection. That moment is really incapable of representation for no human eye witnessed it. The guards were in a dull and deadening sleep when the stone keeping the Lord safely in the hold of the tomb was moved aside. Here we have a contrast with the miracle of Lazarus' rising: in the sight of a multitude the servant came forth at the command of the Lord of life and death. That same Lord arose in a moment imperceptible to all, beyond anyone's gaze.

Christ in his resurrection is prefigured in the Old Testament by Samson (Judg. 16:3) who took hold of the gates of the city of Gaza, put them on his shoulder, and carried them to a Judean hilltop. Jonas, too, stands as a figure of Christ, for after three days and three nights in the belly of the whale he stood on dry land. Early Christian representations in the second century depicted the resurrection by showing Jonas coming forth from the whale. In the third century the mystery was expressed by showing the appearance of the angel to the holy women, the *myrrhophorae,* or bearers of myrrh, at the tomb. By the sixth century the "harrowing of hell," as shown here, was the form used by iconographers to illustrate this unfathomable event in the Lord's life. Thus we see that the feast came to be surrounded with icons showing two moments: the descent into Hades which precedes the actual resurrection and one of the moments following the resurrection, the coming of the holy women to the tomb. Of the latter moment, the Church, in a collect-hymn

for the feast, sings:

> Before the break of dawn,
> the ointment-bearing women
> hastened to the Sun,
> who existed before the sun was made
> but disappeared for a while in the tomb.

The Divine Liturgy of Holy Saturday already carries the theme of the risen Lord, with emphasis on redemption from the power of Hades. Whereas Christ's body is still in the tomb in the slumber of death, he triumphs over the powers that have held captive the righteous people of the Old Covenant. The indestructible bonds that held souls prisoners broke apart when Christ went down into the deepest regions of the earth!

> . . . the tombs also were opened, and many bodies of the saints who had fallen asleep were raised, and coming out of the tombs after his resurrection they went into the holy city and appeared to many (Matthew 27:52f).

The blessing of the new light puts on the lips of Hades an admission of defeat:

> My might has gone, the Shepherd was crucified but now he has awakened Adam. I am deprived of all who were my prisoners. All those I must release who were devoured by me. The graves were vacated by the Crucified and nothing, but nothing, is the value of Death's power.

The deliverance of Adam from hell is indissolubly linked with the redemption. The Second Person of the Godhead had assumed Adam's nature in the downward movement of the incarnation. Adam was dead, and so Christ must assume such *kenosis* to its very limits. Only thus would he draw Adam and, with him, all mankind into the upward sweep of a new creation, into the grand recapitulation of all things, returning to the God from whom they came and to whom they are destined to return.

In the icon Christ is in sheol but definitely as its Vanquisher, not as the vanquished. In iconography a scroll indicates preaching. Here the scroll Christ carries symbolizes his preaching the resurrection to "the spirits in prison" (1 Peter 3:19). The human face of Christ radiates divine gentleness as he bends forward to take Adam by the hand. Eve is already on her feet, or sometimes kneeling, with her hands joined in prayer. The toppled gates of hell upon which

Christ stands have fallen apart in the form of a Cross. The broken locks of the gates lie in the cavernous pit where angels bend over the prince of darkness, ready to bind him in eternal chains forged by the victory of the Prince of Life.

Behind Adam stands the forerunner of Christ, John the Baptist, who points to the victorious Lamb. Kings David and Solomon stand to welcome the Lord who brings forgiveness of sins. Prophets, recognizing the one whose coming they had announced, stand behind Mother Eve. Above the blue *mandorla* or symbol of divine glory, stands a Cross, a mark of Christ's sacrifice and the salvation that streams from it. One of the angels holds a chalice, a reminder of the same. Behind Christ is a triple circle, the symbol of the universe.

The first sheaf of the wheat harvest symbolizes all the bundles to come. The raising of Adam is a sign to us of the resurrection of the body. As the first sheaf of the harvest in the Old Dispensation was gleaned solely for the glory of Yahweh, the God of the harvest, and was burned in the temple, so Christ, the pure wheat and the first sheaf of a harvest yet to come, rose from the dead in a manner too precious for our comprehension, yet not too obscure to be the very core of our songs of praise and adoration. A renewed creation awaiting the fullness of redemption is now a reality, consecrated in the fire of the Spirit. In one of the canticles of the Holy Night, this new people is addressed:

> With lamps in hand, let us go forth to Christ rising from the tomb, as we would go to a bridegroom, and with the feasting multitude, let us celebrate the saving Passover of our God. . . . Let us drink a new drink, produced miraculously not from a barren rock, but springing from the tomb which is the fountain of immortality: the tomb of Christ by which we are strengthened.

In the texts of the liturgy and in the spirituality of the Eastern Church, there is a significant parallel between the nativity and the resurrection, as this ode of an Easter canon points out:

> Having preserved the seals intact, O Christ, thou hast risen from the tomb, and having left unbroken the seals of the immaculate Virgin in thy nativity, thou hast opened to us the gates of paradise.

Here are two ineffable mysteries hidden from all except those who have the eyes of faith. Judith Stoughton, C. S. J., in an article on the nativity, asks:

> Did the Lord's birth prefigure his burial? In the *kenosis* of the Godhead, his abasement, he comes down to take on the weakness of our human nature in the dark womb of a human mother, and accepts it to the very death of that same body. His human life completely emptied, the holy body came to rest in the darkness of the earth-womb. The creature enclosed its Creator in this furthest descent.[36]

The author sees in the swaddling bands of the nativity a prefigurement of the winding sheet that enwrapped Jesus in the tomb.

Easter Week is called the New Week or the Bright Week in the Eastern Church. The whole of creation is given new life in the resurrection of the Lord, and the catechumens baptized on the Holy Night wear their white robes for the next seven days. The Royal Doors of the iconostasis, closed at other times, remain wide open all week to celebrate that Christ broke down the doors of hell and opened the gates of heaven. Because he raised us up from dejection, sin, and sadness, no one kneels during this time, not even in private prayer; the new man stands in the joy of his new life in Christ. There is neither fast nor abstinence from this time until the feast of the Ascension, a literal interpretation of the words of Jesus:

> Can you make wedding guests fast while the bridegroom is with them? The days will come, when the bridegroom is taken from them, and then they will fast in those days (Luke 5:34f).

A Russian writer, Nicolas Zernov, comments: "Only those who have been present at this service can realize all that the resurrection means to the Russian people." In *The Russians and Their Church,* he tells us:

> Every spring a Russian witnesses the resurrection of nature. After six months of immobility and death, life comes back to the Russian land. With noise and triumph, the rivers and lakes burst the ice which has kept them imprisoned for half a year. Grass and flowers appear over-night in the fields, which for many months have been covered with a thick white mantle; the birds begin to sing; the air becomes

scented; men and animals feel exhilarated and reborn. Life proves once more to be stronger than death. This yearly experience of the resurrection of nature has a striking parallel in the history of the Russian people, for, as a nation, they, too, were weighed down, deprived of freedom, overwhelmed for two centuries by the Mongol invader. Then a spring day came; the nation burst its heavy chains and returned to life and light. And this resurrection was achieved by the spiritual force of Christian faith which was mightier than the military skill and numerical strength of the Tartars.

This power of resurrection in nature and history assumed for the Russians its full meaning in the light of Christ's victory over sin and death and therefore Easter is celebrated by them with a joy and splendour unapproached by any other Church. In Russia, not a few devout people only, but the nation as a body has for centuries praised and thanked God for Christ's rising from the tomb. The service on Easter night is an experience which has no parallel in the worship of other nations.[37]

"Christ is risen!" "Indeed, he is risen!!" This exclamation fills the churches, the homes, and the hearts of all devout Eastern Christians during the season. And the Easter canon of St. John Damascene breaks through the darkness of Easter night to declare: "We celebrate the killing of death, the destruction of hell and the dawn of an eternal life."

Chapter 15

The Ascension of the Lord

The Second Book of Kings tells how Elias was taken up to heaven in a fiery chariot while his disciple Eliseus watched. The disciples of Christ likewise witnessed their master ascend to the right hand of the Father.

Ascension is the consummation of the drama of salvation; the birth, death, and resurrection of Jesus are brought to completion in this event in which earth and heaven, the human and the divine, mingle together. Looking at the icon one is struck by the proportionately small area of the picture given to Christ in his moment of ascending: it is, after all, one of his major feasts. The emphasis is on the Mother of God and the disciples and angels. Mary holds the central place. If we read the account of the ascension in the Acts of the Apostles (1:8-11) and in the Synoptics, we see the factual basis for the iconography of the feast. "You shall be my witnesses in Jerusalem and in all Judea and Samaria and to the end of the earth." With these words the Lord defines his Church, its relationship with the world, and its relationship, above all, with himself, with the Father and with the Spirit whom he would send to fill her with power from on high. Thus we see that the emphasis of the feast is not so much on Christ's ascending as it is on the consequences of that event in the life of his body, the Church, and of the world.

The icon is marvelously to the point: Christ is above, seated on a cloud, surrounded by angels. He holds his hand in the position of blessing, a literal representation of the text from Luke, "and lifting up his hands he blessed them. While he blessed them, he parted from them and was carried up into heaven" (24:50f). The glory of Christ is represented by the *mandorla*, the round background that encircles him, a symbol of the heaven above. He now dwells outside the realm of earth and its mode of living; his relationship with his Church and the world is that of one who dwells beyond time and its boundaries. Although the ministering angels, in some icons, appear to lift Christ up or to hold him up, they are there primarily as witnesses of his glory and divinity. He ascended through his own divine strength, needing the assistance of neither man nor angel. In the two distinct parts of the icon, the upper and the lower, the iconographer shows the two separate spheres of heaven and earth.

The Mother of God, the personification of the Church, holds the central place on the icon. She is wrapped in deep tranquillity and purity, sometimes standing in the *orans* position, with arms and hands uplifted in an intercessory posture, and sometimes holding her hands with palms extended upward in front of her, a position used in iconography to depict the profession of faith of martyrs. The stillness of the Virgin, standing in front of the white-robed angels, notes the presence of eternity in time. Her stillness stands out in contrast to the excitement of the apostles on either side of her, each in his own way expressing joy, faith, love, hope. The gesticulations and postures of the apostles indicate the variety of languages and the many ways of expressing truth.

The Mother and the apostles represent the last will of Christ, the inheritance he left to his world. He would not leave this Church, his Bride, alone; he would send to her the Spirit of all fullness, comfort, and enlightenment, and this Spirit would be given not only to those who were physically present at the ascension and Pentecost but also to the Church throughout time. This point is brought out iconographically by the presence among the apostles of St. Paul, who was not actually present at this scene on the Mount of Olives. "I am with you always, to the close of the age." This promise of the Lord, his last words in Matthew's account (28:20), refers, as Ouspensky tells us,

> . . . both to the whole history of the Church in its totality and to each separate member of it until the Second Coming. This is why the gesture of the Saviour is directed towards the group in the foreground whom he is leaving behind and towards the external world. . . . Depicting him in the act of blessing, the icon shows graphically that, even after the Ascension, he remains the source of blessing for the apostles, and through them for their successors and for all those whom they bless. . . . The Lord, while dwelling in heaven, remains not only the source of blessing but also the source of knowledge, communicated to the Church by the Holy Spirit (p. 198).

The following antiphon expresses wonder at the whole incarnate life of Jesus and praises the fruit of that life, the sending of his own Spirit to us:

> O our God, you were born in a manner of your own choosing. You appeared and suffered in the flesh as you willed. You crushed death through your resurrection and ascended into glory; and you sent down the divine Spirit upon us: wherefore we sing a hymn of praise to your divinity and glorify it.

Chapter 16

The Descent of the Holy Spirit

Of old a fire from heaven came down and devoured the holocaust of Elias when he called upon the Lord in the presence of a testy people (1 Kings 18:38). This fire from above was a type of the divine fire that on Pentecost Day came upon the apostles and disciples and made them ready to witness to the Lord and to the power of his resurrection.

Pentecost, the Greek designation for the Old Testament Feast of Weeks, commemorated the giving of the law to Moses on Mount Sinai; it was the occasion when the Israelites gave public thanks for the first fruits of the earth and for the current harvest. The first wheat sheaf was offered to the Lord of the harvest in grateful recollection of his benefits. The Christian feast of Pentecost, fifty days after Easter, inaugurates a new harvest and commemorates the new covenant made by God with his people. His law is written in their minds and on their hearts as the Spirit descends in fire upon the assembled apostles and disciples.

In the Eastern Church the day of Pentecost is the specific festival of the Trinity. On this day the icon of the Holy Trinity, not that of Pentecost, is prominently displayed in church. For this reason the Trinity icon is sometimes called the icon of Pentecost. Pentecost Monday is "Spirit Day." On this day the icon of the descent of the Spirit is specially venerated. It is this icon that we reflect upon here.

With the ascension of Christ and the sending of the Holy Spirit upon the disciples, the work of the Spirit began. "And suddenly a sound came from heaven like the rush of a mighty wind, and it filled all the house where they were sitting" (Acts 2:2). The Pentecost icon conveys harmony and a deep quiet. There is an absence of commotion, a testimony to the peace brought by the mighty wind, and no sign of the disarray of drunkenness of which the disciples were suspected. The apostles sit around a semi-circular table, some of them turning toward one another in conversation. The twelve men pictured in this icon include some not belonging, strictly speaking, to the group of the twelve apostles. This is deliberate; it shows that the Spirit descended not only on the twelve chosen apostles but is given to all the members of the Church. By now Matthias has taken the place left vacant by the defection of Judas, the "lover of silver." Mary, the Mother of Jesus, is not pictured in the icon—is it an indication of belief that fullness of the Spirit was already hers?

The evangelists hold books in their hands, while others carry scrolls, a symbol of their office as preachers of the Word. Upon all of them rays or tongues of fire descend from heaven, signified by a circle that extends beyond the edge of the icon. The icon conveys a general impression of unity even though the various postures and individual characteristics indicate diversity; it is the one Spirit who disperses an abundance and variety of gifts and operations. At the center of the picture is an unoccupied place. Christ is the head of the Church and dwells with her although he is not visibly present.

At the lower center of the icon is an interesting figure bearing the inscription "Cosmos"—an old man with a crown on his head. This feature is peculiar to the East and is not known in the West's portrayal of Pentecost. Who is this little man, and what is his role? N. Pokrovsky in *The Gospels in Iconographic Records*, quoted in Leonid Ouspensky's treatment of the feast, writes:

> The man sits in a dark place, since the whole world had formerly been without faith; he is bowed down with years, for he was made old by the sin of Adam; his red garment signifies the devil's blood sacrifices; the royal crown signifies sin, which ruled in the world; the white cloth in his hands with the twelve scrolls means the twelve apostles, who brought light to the whole world with their teaching (p. 209).

In some icons the prophet Joel replaces the little man Cosmos. It was Joel who foretold the coming of the Spirit upon all mankind, men and women, young and old.

One of the collect hymns or *kondaks* for the feast of Pentecost contrasts the feast with the tower of Babel event:

> When the All-Highest, descending, confounded the tongues, he divided the nations; but when he distributed the tongues of fire at Pentecost, he called all men to unity; wherefore with one accord we glorify the All-holy Spirit.

At Babel the peoples lost the unity of speech and were scattered by their building of an earthly tower; now they recover this unity and are gathered together "in the spiritual building of the Church, fused into its single holy body by the fire of love" (Ouspensky, p. 208).

The deep unity that is communicated through this icon is a reflection of the oneness in the Trinity. This unity in the bond of the Spirit is what the Bride of Christ, the Church, is called to attain through the love and grace of the Spirit poured forth into her heart. Gertrud von Le Fort puts on the lips of the Church these words:

> Jubilation is my name
>   and rejoicing is my countenance,
> I am like a young meadow
> wreathed in dawn. . . .
> I bloom in the red-thorn of His love,
>   I bloom on all my branches
>   in the purple of His gifts.
> I bloom with fiery tongues,
>   I bloom with flaming fulfilment,
>   I bloom out of the Holy Spirit of God
>   (p. 49).

The ecclesiological meaning of Pentecost is deeply, indissolubly linked with the central truth of Christianity, the Trinity.

Chapter 17

The Holy Trinity

The Eastern Church, unlike the West, has no specific day for celebrating a feast in honor of the Blessed Trinity. Nevertheless, some of the finest visual expressions of this most profound mystery are found in the homes, churches, and monasteries of our Eastern brethren.

On the feast of Pentecost the mystery of the Trinity is in the forefront, while on Pentecost Monday, the Church observes "Spirit Day." In iconography and art in general the portrayal of the Trinity has a complicated history. Intricate problems face any artist attempting a work on the Trinity for in itself this mystery is undepictable. From very early times and for many centuries, the historical biblical scene of the three visitors to Abraham and Sarah under the oak of Mamre (Gen. 18) was the only representation of the Trinity. This scene is still preserved in the Eastern Church for its concordance with the doctrine of the Trinity. Fully corresponding with this doctrine in its artistic expression is the masterpiece by Andrei Rublev (*ca.* 1370-1430). Many consider his icon to be one of the most perfect achievements in the history of art. By the Middle Ages, Russian art had three iconographical variations depicting the Holy Trinity: the "Old Testament Trinity" portrayed the three visitors to Abraham and Sarah; the "Paternity" showed the venerable Father holding on his lap a young beardless Christ who in turn holds an orb adorned with a white dove, the Holy Spirit; the "New Testament Trinity" showed Father and Son seated on thrones while hovering over them was the Holy Spirit.

How does it happen that the "Old Testament Trinity" was preferred to the others since the revelation of the Trinity was not made in the Old Testament but belongs specifically to the New Testament? Many events, persons, and passages of the Old Testament are seen to be types, foreshadowings of New Testament events and persons. One such account is recorded in the eighteenth chapter of Genesis. Abraham and Sarah are hosts to three visitors, commonly called "angels." Abraham begs the travelers to stay in his tent at Mamre while he prepares food for their refreshment on the journey ahead.

The New Testament parallels present themselves quite clearly. The angels on their way through Mamre had foretold to Abraham and Sarah the marvelous birth of a son, Isaac. An archangel bore to the Virgin Mary the news of the miraculous birth of the Son of God. In the great test put to his faith, Abraham received the command of God to sacrifice his only son, Isaac. Like a meek lamb Isaac walked with his father to the place of sacrifice. In perfect obedience to the Father, Jesus, his only son, willingly offered his life on the Cross for the salvation of the world.

Each Person of the Blessed Trinity takes part in the plan of Divine Providence for the world, each with his own specific manifestation. A hymn used at Great Vespers emphasizes the distinctness of the divine Persons and, at the same time, the unity of their nature as one God. We proclaim the Father as "doing all things through the Son with the participation of the Holy Spirit." We confess the Son, our Redeemer, "through whom we have known the Father and through whom the Holy Spirit came into the world." And we profess our faith in the Spirit as the Person "giving life to all living things."

The descent of the Spirit upon the world revealed to man the mystery of the Trinity, one in substance, undivided, and yet distinct. At the baptism of Jesus the revelation of the Trinity was impinged upon the external senses of those present; in the feast of Pentecost, man, by the power of the Spirit, is endowed with the possibility of participating in the life of God, Father, Son, and Holy Spirit, and of becoming a dwelling place of divine light, love, and grace. This new life that is brought by the Spirit is the cause of great rejoicing. The Eastern Church responds to this call by decorating their churches and homes with an abundance of branches, flowers, and plants. During the Divine Liturgy on Pentecost Day, the faithful carry flowers as a sign of the blossoming of all things and their renewal in the power of the indwelling Spirit.

In Rublev's icon of the Trinity we see the house of Abraham and the oak of Mamre. In his portrayal of the scene, Rublev omitted all nonessential figures and details. By doing so he directs our attention to the spiritual meaning of the event, particularly to the significance of the three visitors. The basic compositional form of Rublev's icon of the Trinity, distinct from other painters' interpretations, is the circle. The angels sit so close that their wings are touching. An art historian, M. Alpatov, in his book *Andrei Rublev* speaks of this circular movement:

> Rublev breathed new content into this old theme [the Trinity]. His three angels personify the longing of the Russian people for the peace and harmony so vainly to be sought in the life of those times. And how happy the forms in which this longing is expressed, enchanting in their amazing unity, their essentially musical harmony! The circle—there we have the leitmotif of the entire composition. We find it in the bowed figure of the angel on the right, in the outlines of the mountain and the tree, in the inclination of the central angel's head, in the parabolic lines prevailing in the figure of the angel on the left, in the placing of the pedestals. The wonderful compositional rhythm of the icon is enhanced by the colouring which is musical beyond all words. Amity—such would be the most appropriate term for the colour scheme of the icon, so clear, so lucid, so transparent; for it expresses with remarkable force the amity, the harmony among the three angels.[38]

Dionysius the Areopagite also speaks of the

significance of the circle in his treatise *On Divine Names*, quoted by Ouspensky:

> . . . circular movement signifies that God remains identical with Himself, that He envelops in synthesis the intermediate parts and the extremities, which are at the same time containers and contained, and that He recalls to Himself all that has gone forth from Him (p. 203).

In Rublev's icon the angels at each side of the table lean toward the angel in the center. Through the circular curve of their bodies and heads, a unity of form and movement is created. The hands of all three gesture toward the dish containing the sacrificial animal, which is considered a symbol of the Eucharist. The vessel containing the consecrated food stands on the table as on an altar. This signifies the unity of will and action in the Persons of the Trinity. The faces and features of the three show a recognizable similarity. Pictorially this indicates that the angels represent the Trinity, are indissolubly united, and possess eternal youth and beauty in common. While the similarity of the figures is emphasized, at the same time each has its own individuality of attitude and expression. This denotes the distinctness of each divine Person and also points to the differences of activity attributed to each in the creation, redemption, and sanctification of the world.

From left to right, the angels are types of the Father, the Son, and the Consoler Spirit. The Father appears to be grieving; he inspires the Son to obey in the face of sacrifice, while he himself painfully surrenders his only Son to the free will of sinners so that, through his perfect sacrifice, they might all be redeemed. Because the Father cannot be seen by our bodily eyes, Rublev has chosen indistinct shades of coloring for his clothing. The outer cloak is an indefinite, sober color and his other garment is pale pink with lights of pale green and brown. It does not hold our attention, a fact that has an interesting parallel in the brevity with which we profess in the Creed our belief in the Person of the Father Almighty, acknowledging him simply as "Maker of heaven and earth."

The Holy Spirit blesses the cup along with Christ. The properties of the Third Person are such that they revivify and renew all things in love. For this reason the Spirit is garbed in light green as a symbol of youthfulness and fullness of powers. The Son in the center blesses the cup, indicating thereby his readiness to offer himself as a Lamb in sacrifice, to die in atonement for the sins of mankind. His head is bowed in submission to the Father. Because the divine Son became man and because we have seen his face at a precise historical moment in time, he is clothed in precise, clear colors—a purple-brown and bright blue. This precise coloring of the central figure contrasts with the soft, less distinct colors of the others, and yet there is a color common to the clothing of all three—the blue that makes them sparkle with brightness.

The unification brought about by the coloring and by the compositional rhythm of the circular motif reveals the mastery with which Rublev addressed himself to the mystery of a single nature in the three divine Persons. A good measure of the enchantment, deep beauty and charm of this icon consists in that the artist has delivered us from the elderly, white-bearded representation of the Father and has also put into the frame of human beauty and youth the image of the Third Person, in contrast to the dove form.

Rublev, the monk, was commissioned by the abbot of Trinity Monastery in Zagorsk to do this work in order that the monks might overcome their fear of a world torn apart by hate and that they might find in the contemplation of the mystery portrayed a divine source for their longing for amity and concord. During the Divine Liturgy of St. John Chrysostom the choir sings of the harmony that precedes and flows from professing faith in the Holy Trinity:

> Let us love one another, so that with one mind we may profess the Father, the Son and the Holy Spirit—Trinity—one in substance and undivided.

Our reflections on the icon of the Trinity form an appropriate conclusion to this book, for this mystery precedes, follows, and utterly envelops the entire life of man.

> Great God of my life, I will praise Thee
> on the three shores of Thy one light.
> I will plunge with my song into the sea
> of Thy glory:
> with rejoicing into the waves
> of Thy power. . . .
> Be praised for all that lives.
> God of Thy Son, great God of
> Thine eternal compassion,

great God of Thine erring humanity,
God of all them who suffer,
   God of all them who die,
    brotherly God on our dark spoor:
I thank Thee that Thou has delivered us,
  I thank Thee to the choirs
    of Thine angels.
Be praised for our blessedness!
God of Thine own Spirit,
   flooding in Thy depths from love to love,
Seething down into my soul. . . .

Holy Creator of Thy new earth:
I thank Thee that I may thank Thee, Lord,
  I thank Thee to the choirs
    of Thine angels. . . .
I will sing Thy praises on the three shores
    of Thy one light.
I will plunge with my song into the sea
    of Thy glory:
  with shouts of joy into the waves of
    of Thy power
      (von Le Fort, "Te Deum," pp. 51-2).

NOTES

1 Vladimir Soloukhin, *Searching for Icons in Russia,* trans. Helen and Kurt Wolff (New York: Harcourt, Brace, Jovanovich, 1972), pp. 149-50.

2 Quoted by Aristeides Papadakis, "The Theological Premise of Byzantine Iconography," *John XXIII Lectures: 1966 Byzantine Christian Heritage, II* (New York: John XXIII Center for Eastern Christian Studies, 1969), p. 51.

3 *Ibid.,* p. 54.

4 *Ibid.*

5 Johannes Quasten, *Patrology: The Beginnings of Patristic Literature* (Westminster, Maryland: The Newman Press, 1949), cf. pp. 106-57.

6 Leonid Ouspensky and Vladimir Lossky, *The Meaning of Icons,* trans. G.E.H. Palmer and E. Kadloubovsky (Boston: Boston Book and Art Shop, 1952), p. 33.

7 Philip Sherrard, "The Art of the Icon," *Sacrament and Image: Essays in the Christian Understanding of Man,* ed. A.M. Allchin (London: The Fellowship of S. Alban and S. Sergius, 1967), p. 58.

8 London: Methuen & Co. Ltd., 1965, cf. p. 24.

9 Ouspensky and Lossky, *op.cit.* p. 40. (Hereafter referred to in the text.)

10 Nicholas of Cusa, *The Vision of God,* trans. Emma Gurney Salter, intro. by Evelyn Underhill (New York: Frederick Ungar Publishing Co., 2nd printing, 1969), p. xii. (Permission to quote from J.M. Dent & Sons Ltd., London.)

11 New York: Viking Press, 1963, cf. p. 107.

12 John A. Goodall, "Icons and Spirituality: an Essay in Interpretation," *One in Christ,* Vol. IX: 3 (1973), p. 290.

13 A.M. Allchin, "Creation, Incarnation, Interpretation," *Sacrament and Image,* ed. A.M. Allchin, p. 51.

14 All further quotations unaccounted for in this book indicate material from the Divine Liturgy and/or the Hours of the Eastern Church. Excerpts from *Byzantine Daily Worship* by Most Rev. Joseph Raya and Baron José de Vinck are used by permission of the Alleluia Press, Allendale, New Jersey.

15 Ivan Kologrivov, trans. Sr. Electa, O.C.D., "Psychological Foundations of Russian Sanctity, " *Desert Call* (published by the Spiritual Life Institute of America, Sedona, Arizona), Vol. 8, No. 3 (1973).

16 Roger Fry, "Russian Icon Painting from a Western-European Point of View," *Masterpieces of Russian Painting,* ed. M. Farbman (London: Europa Publications Ltd., 1931), pp. 36, 38, 46.

17 Metropolitan Anthony Bloom, "Body and Matter in Spiritual Life," Allchin, ed., *op. cit.,* p. 37.

18 Nicolas Zernov, *The Russians and Their Church* (London: S.P.C.K., 1954, published for The Fellowship of S. Alban and S. Sergius), pp. 107-8.

19 Irene Posnoff, "Russia," *The Soul of the Nations,* coll. by Gabriel Boutsen, O.F.M. (Milwaukee: Bruce Publishing Co., 1960), pp. 34-5.

20 Quasten, *op. cit.,* p. 212.

21 Gertrud von Le Fort, trans. Margaret Chanler, *Hymns to the Church* (New York: Sheed and Ward, 1953), "Christmas," p. 40.

22 C. S. Lewis, *Miracles, a Preliminary Study* (New York: Macmillan Company, 1947), p. 112.

23 In the Divine Liturgy of St. John Chrysostom, the deacon represents the angel, symbolically repeating the gesture of one wing raised in flight. The deacon lifts his stole with his right hand each time he calls the faithful to prayer. The flight of the angel is from heaven to earth, while the call of the deacon is addressed to the devout to lift themselves from earth to heaven in prayer (cf. Ouspensky, p. 174).

24 Thomas Drain, "The Cave of the Nativity," *Sacred Signs,* No. 6--Vol. 2, Nos. 3 & 4, Christmas (1963), p. 66.

25 Judith Stoughton, C.S.J., "Swaddling Clothes and Linen Bands: from the Manger to the Tomb," *ibid.,* p. 50.

26 Ade Bethune, "The Ox and the Ass at the Manger," *ibid.*, p. 62.

27 Margaret Mooney, trans., "Hail Blessed Flower!" (St. Paul: North Central Publishing Co., 1973), p. 19.

28 Kenneth Patchen, "I Have Lighted the Candles, Mary," *Collected Poems* (New York: New Directions Publishing Corporation, 1942), p. 177.

29 Robert Herrick, "A Christmas Carol, Sung to the King in the Presence at Whitehall," public domain, but printed in *A Wreath of Christmas Poems*, ed. Albert M. Hayes and James Laughlin (New York: New Directions Publishing Corporation, 1972).

30 In very early Christianity a man's age was determined from the time of his baptism, his birth unto new life, rather than from the time of his natural birth. In the catacombs baptized persons were depicted as children.

31 In the court of Byzantium the hands of courtiers were covered out of deep respect whenever they received anything from or handed something to the emperor. Reverence before something holy is portrayed in this way in iconography, for example, Simeon and Joseph in the presentation of Christ in the temple, the angels in the baptism of Jesus, etc.

32 Dame Aemiliana Lohr, *The Mass through the Year,* Vol, I, Advent to Palm Sunday (Westminster, Maryland: The Newman Press, 1958), pp. 171-2.

33 Lewis, *op. cit.*, p. 156.

34 The information on the Office of the burial of Christ and the morning Office of Great Friday comes from a personal communication with the Very Rev. Laurence Mancuso of New Skete, the Monks of the Brotherhood of St. Francis, Cambridge, New York.

35 St. Gregory the Theologian, *Easter Sermon 45,* quoted by Ouspensky, p. 186.

36 Stoughton, *op. cit.,* p. 49.

37 Nicolas Zernov, *The Russians and Their Church* (London: S.P.C.K., 3rd ed., 1964), pp. 178-9.

38 M. Alpatov, *Andrei Rublev* (Moscow-Leningrad, 1943).

Alexeev, Wassilij and Theofanis Stavrou, *The Great Revival: the Russian Church under German Occupation.* Minneapolis: Burgess Publishing Co., 1976.

Allchin, A.M. ed. *Sacrament and Image: Essays in the Christian Understanding of Man.* London: The Fellowship of S. Alban and S. Sergius, 1967.

Alpatov, M. *Andrei Rublev.* Moscow-Leningrad, 1943.

_____. *Art Treasures of Russia,* trans. Norbert Guterman. New York: Harry N. Abrams, Inc.

Arseniev, Nicholas. *Russian Piety,* trans. Asheleigh Moorhouse. The Library of Orthodox Theology, No. 3. London: The Faith Press Ltd., 1964.

Bethune, Ade. "The Ox and the Ass at the Manger." *Sacred Signs,* Christmas, 1963, pp. 57-62.

Biederman, Hermengild M., ed. *The Passion.* Pictorial Library of Eastern Church Art, Vol. 2, trans. Hans Hermann Rosenwald. Catholic Art Book Guild, 1964.

Billington, James H. *The Icon and the Axe: An Interpretive History of Russian Culture.* New York: Random House, Inc., Vintage Books, 1970.

Brianchaninov, Ignatius. *On the Prayer of Jesus.* London: John M. Watkins, 1965.

Conway, Sir Martin. "The History of Russian Icon Painting." *Masterpieces of Russian Painting,* ed. M. Farbman. London: Europa Publications Ltd., 1931.

Curtiss, John Shelton. *The Russian Church and the Soviet State: 1917-1950.* Boston: Little, Brown and Company, 1953.

Didron, Adolphe Napoleon. *Christian Iconography.* Vol.II, trans. E.J. Millington; completed and added to by Margaret Stokes. New York: Frederick Ungar Publishing Co., 1st ed. 1886; republished 1965.

Drain, Thomas A. "The Cave of the Nativity." *Sacred Signs,* Christmas, 1963, pp. 64-8.

Fabricius, Ulrich. *Icons: Portrayals of Christ,* trans. Hans Hermann Rosenwald. Pictorial Library of Eastern Church Art, Vol. 9. Recklinghausen, West Germany: Aurel Bongers, 1967.

Farbman, M., ed. *Masterpieces of Russian Painting.* London: Europa Publications Ltd., 1931.

Fedotov, G.P., ed. *A Treasury of Russian Spirituality.* London: Sheed and Ward, 1950, 2nd ed. 1952.

French, R.M. *The Eastern Orthodox Church.* London: Hutchinson's University Library, 1951.

Fry, Roger. "Russian Icon Painting from a Western-European Point of View." *Masterpieces of Russian Painting,* ed. M. Farbman. London: Europa Publications Ltd., 1931.

Goodall, John A. "Icons and Spirituality: an Essay in Interpretation." *One in Christ.* Vol. IX: 3, 1973, pp. 284-93.

Hackel, Alexei A. *The Icon,* trans. Sergei Hackel. Herder Art Series. Freiburg im Breisgau, West Germany, 1954.

Hare, Richard. *The Art and Artists of Russia.* Greenwich, Conn.: New York Graphic Society, 1965.

Iswolsky, Helene. *Christ in Russia: The History, Tradition, and Life of the Russian Church.* Milwaukee: Bruce Publishing Co., 1960.

Keim, Jean A. *Russian Icons.* Petite Encyclopédie de l'Art, Vol. 86. New York: Tudor Publishing Co., 1967.

Kologrivov, Ivan. "Psychological Foundations of Russian Sanctity," trans. Sr. Electa, O.C.D. *Desert Call,* Vol. 8, No. 3, 1973.

Kornilovich, Kira. *Arts of Russia: From the Origins to the End of the 16th Century,* trans. James Hogarth. Cleveland and New York: World Publishing Company, 1967.

Lasareff, Victor. *Russian Icons from the Twelfth to the Fifteenth Century.* New York: New American Library of World Literature, Inc., 1967.

McDowell, Bart and Conger, Dean. *Journey Across Russia: The Soviet Union Today.* Washington, D.C.: National Geographic Society, 1977.

Mathew, Gervase. *Byzantine Aestheticism.* New York: Viking Press, 1963.

Monk of the Eastern Church. *Jesus: A Dialogue with the Savior.* Paris: Desclée Co., 1967.

_____. *The Prayer of Jesus.* Paris: Desclée Co., 1967.

_____. *On the Invocation of the Name of Jesus.* London: The Fellowship of S. Alban and S. Sergius, 1950.

Nicholas of Cusa. *The Vision of God,* trans. Emma Gurney Salter. New York: Frederick Ungar Publishing Co., 1928, republished 1960.

Obolensky, Dmitri. *The Byzantine Commonwealth: Eastern Europe, 500-1453.* London: Weidenfelde and Nicolson, 1971.

Ouspensky, Leonid and Lossky, Vladimir. *The Meaning of Icons,* trans. G.E.H. Palmer and E. Kadloubovsky. Boston: Boston Book and Art Shop, 1952.

Papadakis, Aristeides. "The Theological Premise of Byzantine Iconography." *John XXIII Lectures: 1966 Byzantine Christian Heritage,* Vol. II, 1969.

Papaioannou, Kostas. *Byzantine and Russian Painting,* trans. Janet Sondheimer. New York: Funk & Wagnalls, 1965.

Posnoff, Irene. "Russia." *The Soul of the Nations,* ed. Gabriel Boutsen, O.F.M. Milwaukee: Bruce Publishing Co., 1960. pp. 28-37.

Putnam, Mother C.E. "The Image as Sacramental." *Sacrament and Image: Essays in the Christian Understanding of Man.* ed. A.M. Allchin. London: The Fellowship of S. Alban and S. Sergius, 1967. pp. 12-6.

Rice, David Talbot. *Byzantine Icons.* London: Faber and Faber, 1959.

_____. *Byzantine Painting: The Last Phase.* New York: The Dial Press, 1968.

Rice, Tamara Talbot. *Icons.* London: Batchworth Press.

_____. *Russian Icons.* New York: Marboro Books, 1963.

St. Leo League Publications. *Sacred Signs.* Newport, Rhode Island.

Schmemann, Alexander. "Liturgical Spirituality of the Sacraments." *John XXIII Lectures: 1966 Christian Heritage,* Vol. II, 1969, pp. 19-33.

Sherrard, Philip. "The Art of the Icon." *Sacrament and Image: Essays in the Christian Understanding of Man,* ed. A.M. Allchin. London: The Fellowship of S. Alban and S. Sergius, 1967. pp. 12-6.

Soloukin, Vladimir. *Searching for Icons in Russia,* trans. Helen and Kurt Wolff. New York: Harcourt, Brace, Jovanovich, 1972.

Stoughton, Judith, C.S.J. "Swaddling Clothes and Linen Bands: from the Manger to the Tomb." *Sacred Signs,* Christmas, 1963, pp. 49-51.

Trubetskoi, Eugene N. *Icons, Theology in Color.* Crestwood, New York: St. Vladimir Seminary Press, 1973.

UNESCO World Art Series. *USSR Early Russian Icons,* ed. Victor Lasareff and Otto Demus. Greenwich, Conn.: New York Graphic Society, 1958.

Ware, Kallistos Timothy. "The Transfiguration of the Body." *Sacrament and Image: Essays in the Christian Understanding of Man,* ed. A.M. Allchin. London: The Fellowship of S. Alban and S. Sergius, 1967. pp. 17-32.

Weitzmann, Kurt, *et al. A Treasury of Icons: Sixth to Seventeenth Centuries* (from the Sinai Peninsula, Greece, Bulgaria and Yugoslavia), trans. Robert Erich Wolf. New York: Harry N. Abrams, Inc., 1966.

Winkler, Martin. *Holidays of the Church.* Pictorial Library of Eastern Church Art, Vol. 8. Recklinghausen, West Germany, 1958.

Yevseyeva, L.M., *et al. Early Tver Painting,* trans. Natasha Johnstone. Moscow: Iskusstvo Publishers, 1974.

Zernov, Nicolas. *The Russians and Their Church.* London: S.P.C.K., 3rd ed., 1964.